THE GRASMERE JOURNAL

THE GRASMERE JOURNAL

Dorothy Wordsworth

the revised and complete text
with an introduction by Jonathan Wordsworth

HENRY HOLT AND COMPANY
NEW YORK

Published in the United States by
Henry Holt and Company, Inc., 521 Fifth Avenue,
New York, New York 10175

This illustrated edition was conceived, designed and produced by
The Albion Press Limited, 9 Stewart Street, Oxford, OX1 4RH,
in association with The Wordsworth Trust, Dove Cottage, Grasmere.

Library of Congress Catalog Card Number: 87-80631

ISBN 0-8050-0630-3

First American Edition

Designer: Emma Bradford
Editor: Jane Havell
Picture Researcher: Elizabeth Loving

Printed in Great Britain

1 3 5 7 9 10 8 6 4 2

HALF-TITLE: *Dove Cottage, Town End, Grasmere, by Dora Wordsworth
after Amos Green*
TITLE PAGE: *Dorothy Wordsworth, after Samuel Crosthwaite, 1833*

ISBN 0-8050-0630-3

Contents

Introduction

'William and John', *The Grasmere Journal* begins, 'set off into Yorkshire after dinner at half past two o'clock, cold pork in their pockets.' It seems very ordinary, very factual, but at once we feel a confidence in the person who is writing. Her precision about the time suggests that she is to be trusted, and the cold pork is one of countless little details that will tell us of the frugal, unpretentious life that was lived at Dove Cottage. Dorothy's thoughts revolve about her brothers – William, the poet, especially; and John, who was a sea-captain, home on leave between voyages to the East. At this moment they have 'set off into Yorkshire' because at Gallow Hill Farm, near Scarborough, Mary Hutchinson (one of Dorothy's oldest friends, and William's future wife) is keeping house for her brother Tom.

Dorothy, born on Christmas Day 1771, was eighteen months younger than William. On the death of their mother in 1778 she had been sent to live with relatives, on the grounds that a female child could not properly grow up in an all-male household. Though she met her brothers from time to time over the years, it was not until April 1794 that she realised her ambition of setting up house with William – and then only for six weeks. Meanwhile William had had an undistinguished career at Cambridge, 1787–91, twice visited France (1790 and 1791–2), and published two considerable poems, 'An Evening Walk' and 'Descriptive Sketches'. He had also been converted to the ideals of the French Revolution, and become the father of a French child, baptised in Orleans Cathedral on 15 December 1792 as Anne-Caroline Wordsworth.

Because of the war with France, it was ten years before Wordsworth was able once again to meet Caroline's mother, Annette Vallon. How long he continued to assume that they would be married we cannot know. Her two surviving letters, however (confiscated by the French police in March 1793, and rediscovered in 1922), are full of tenderness, and show an entire confidence that love is shared. Interestingly, the longer and more emotional of the two is addressed to Dorothy, and it is taken for granted that they will all live together.

Annette's dream was not to be. The war dragged on; her letters became rarer; Dorothy's importance in her brother's life increased as his thoughts turned gradually back to Nature, and away from politics. It was Dorothy who helped Wordsworth through a period of breakdown in spring 1796, Dorothy who (in the words of his great autobiographical poem, 'The Prelude'):

> in the midst of all, preserved me still
> A poet, made me seek beneath that name
> My office upon earth, and nowhere else.

After two years spent at Racedown in Dorset, they moved in July 1797 to Alfoxden, Somerset, to be near Coleridge in the village of Nether Stowey. It was to be one of the most inspired of all literary companionships. Coleridge wrote his three great 'magical' poems, 'Kubla Khan', 'The Ancient Mariner' and 'Christabel' Part One; Wordsworth wrote 'The Thorn', 'The Idiot Boy', 'Tintern Abbey', and much else; Dorothy composed the first of her Journals (never printed in full, and now sadly lost), telling of walks on the Quantock Hills, and evoking the marvellous closeness of their relationship – 'three persons, and one soul'.

Following the year with Coleridge in Somerset, and the joint publication of *Lyrical Ballads*, came a winter of extreme cold and isolation at Goslar in Germany. Wordsworth wrote the famous 'Lucy' poems and the early scenes of 'The Prelude', but Dorothy, cooped up indoors, had no scope for keeping a journal. Instead, she copied her brother's finished poems into elegant red-leather notebooks – a process that continued, with help from Mary when they returned to England, and went to stay with the Hutchinsons in County Durham. Then, in the very last days of the eighteenth century, William and Dorothy moved into Dove Cottage. The house was rented, but for the first time they had a home that was truly their own.

Dorothy was almost twenty-eight. Old Molly Fisher gives us, in her broad Cumbrian dialect, a picture of her, standing in front of the parlour-fire at Dove Cottage on the day of their arrival (20 December 1799): 'I mun never forget t'laal striped gown and t'laal straw bonnet, as ye stood here.' It was mid-winter, and they had walked almost the whole way across the country; the little striped dress and straw bonnet would have done good service. Apart from a silhouette, which came to light in 1965, there is no portrait of Dorothy as a young woman. Coleridge, however, offers a fascinating description in July 1797. He has known her under a month:

> Wordsworth and his exquisite sister are with me. She is a woman indeed! – in mind, I mean, and heart . . . if you expected to see a pretty woman, you would think her ordinary; if you expected to find an ordinary woman, you would find her pretty! But her manners are simple, ardent, impressive . . . her eye watchful in minutest observation of nature, and her taste a perfect electrometer – it bends, protrudes, and draws in, at subtlest beauties and most recondite faults.

The Grasmere Journal was begun, as Dorothy said, 'because I shall give William pleasure by it when he comes home again'. It extends from 14 May 1800 to 16 January 1803, with a gap of almost a year (22 December 1800–9 October 1801), where a notebook has been lost. To it we owe an immense amount of information about the writing of Wordsworth's poetry, and about the life out of which the poetry sprang. Still more important, though, are the riches of Dorothy's prose. She has no thoughts of publication, and the details she describes of everyday life cannot always be of interest, but she has a delight in making phrases that singles her out as a true writer:

> The colours of the mountains soft and rich, with orange fern – the cattle pasturing upon the hill-tops kites sailing in the sky above our heads – sheep bleating and in lines and chains and patterns scattered over the mountains.

Could anything more beautifully conjure up an autumn day on the fells? For those who know the landscape, the reddening bracken, cows high on the hills, hawks overhead, and scattered sheep, will form an instant picture. For those who do not, there is still an extraordinary sense of well-being – of things being as they should. An atmosphere has been created to which it is impossible not to respond. Coleridge once described a hillside as 'speckled thin with sheep'; Dorothy wishes to be more precise. In her final clause we sense the rhythm pausing as she seeks for words that will be true to the 'inward eye': 'in *lines* and *chains* and *patterns* scattered over the mountains'.

Dorothy's world is all alive. Nesting swallows at her window 'twitter and make a bustle and a little cheerful song hanging against the panes of glass, with their soft white bellies . . . and their forked fish-like tails.' 'They swim round and round', she adds, 'and again they come.' Her favourite birch-tree bends to the breezes, 'as if for love of its own delightful motions', and it is the same delight that she notices in a child who is helping a fellow-traveller with his carts: 'Her business seemed to be all pleasure – pleasure in her own motions – and the man looked at her as if he too was pleased and spoke to her in the same tone in which he spoke to his horses.' The tenderness of this last detail is to be found again and again in Dorothy's writing – not least in her account of the daffodils on Ullswater that is the source of her brother's most famous poem:

> When we were in the woods beyond Gowbarrow Park we saw a few daffodils close to the waterside. We fancied that the lake had floated the seeds ashore, and that the little colony had so sprung up. But as we went along there were more and yet more and at last under the boughs of the trees, we saw that there was a long belt of them along the shore, about the breadth of a country turnpike road. I never saw daffodils so beautiful they grew among the mossy stones about and about them, some rested their heads upon these stones as on a pillow for weariness and the rest tossed and reeled and danced and seemed as if they verily laughed with the wind that blew upon them over the lake, they looked so gay ever glancing ever changing.

It is easy to play down Dorothy's achievement – to imply that she is artless, or just (as in Coleridge's up-to-date scientific image of the electrometer) abnormally sensitive to her surroundings. This is far from being the case. Though it retains a wonderful spontaneity, her prose depends quite as much as her brother's poem on the writer's imagination. As we read, it seems utterly natural that the flowers should rest, 'pillow' their heads, feel weariness, dance, and laugh; and yet these metaphors have transformed the landscape, taught us how to see, and feel, and respond. Nor is it a question merely of Dorothy's transferring to the flowers her own human feelings: she can stand back and take a larger view. At the end of her account she takes up her earlier reference to a turnpike road, and develops it into a remarkable image of the highway of life.

To Wordsworth the daffodils are precious as an unfading memory, a part of the life of his own mind:

> They flash upon that inward eye
> Which is the bliss of solitude;
> And then my heart with pleasure fills
> And dances with the daffodils.

For Dorothy, the flowers have a busy life that is all their own:

> This wind blew directly over the lake to them. There was here and there a little knot and a few stragglers a few yards higher up but they were so few as not to disturb the simplicity and unity and life of that one busy highway.

We look back to Dorothy and William Wordsworth with the detachment – almost reverence – that is felt for great writers of the past. It is interesting to ask how they seemed to their neighbours. Dove Cottage had been an inn, The Dove and Olive Bough, and was larger than the half-dozen surrounding cottages. Molly Fisher, who lived opposite, was delighted to be taken on as a servant when the Wordsworths arrived. For 'two or three hours a day', the poet records, she would be paid two shillings a week, plus her food on Saturdays, and when there were visitors. 'We could have had this attendance', he remarks, 'for eighteenpence a week, but we added the sixpence for the sake of the poor woman, who is made happy by it.' At times during the Napoleonic War a four-pound loaf of bread cost more than half Molly's weekly wages: what seemed to Wordsworth a gesture meant a great deal more to her. Yet he and Dorothy were not at all well off themselves. They could afford certain small luxuries that were denied to their neighbours – tea, for instance (still very expensive at this period), and a newspaper – but they rarely bought clothes, they ate little meat, and they were grateful when a relative sent them a barrel of flour from America.

Three events take place during the period of *The Grasmere Journal* that are of great importance: the visit of William and Dorothy in August 1802 to Annette and Caroline at Calais (made possible by the short-lived Peace of Amiens); Wordsworth's marriage in October to Mary Hutchinson; and the settlement in 1803 of a debt of £8,700, owed to the family by Lord Lonsdale, son of their father's late employer. Dorothy does not keep her journal while in France, and when she writes it up on her return we hear nothing of William's and Annette's feelings, or of Caroline's first meeting with her father. She is by no means so reticent over the wedding. In a sentence that was discreetly omitted by her first editors, we learn not only that Dorothy wore the ring herself the night before, but that William, in an acknowledgement of their special relationship, slipped it back onto her finger on the morning itself: 'I gave him the wedding-ring – with how deep a blessing! I took it from my forefinger where I had worn it the whole of the night before – he slipped it again onto my finger, and blessed me fervently.'

Mary and William were both thirty-two, and had known each other since childhood. Before Wordsworth's meeting with Annette they had intended some day to be married, and though it was several years before they saw each other again, Mary clearly accepted what had happened. Similarly, there is never a hint that she is jealous of Dorothy, or Dorothy of her. William is central to both their lives. Of the journey back after the wedding, Dorothy records: 'We had sunshine and showers, pleasant talk, love and cheerfulness.' We may if we choose take the showers to be symbolic, but there is no encouragement to do so. Back in Grasmere four days later, Dorothy writes: 'we baked bread, and Mary and I walked, first upon the hillside, and then in John's Grove, then in view of Rydale, the first walk that I had taken with my sister.'

In one sense it had been a great upheaval; in another, nothing had changed. The following year Dorothy composed her *Recollections of a Tour Made in Scotland*, with its impressive longer passages of description, but increasingly her role became that of second mother to the children. In 1829 she became seriously ill, and from 1835 suffered from arteriosclerosis. She lost the use of her legs, and her brain was affected. After twenty years of appalling sadness, she died in January 1855. Her last period of sanity coincided with the death of her brother on 23 April 1850.

Like William, she had been at the height of her powers in the early Grasmere years, years of 'plain living and high thinking'. She described Dove Cottage in detail in a letter of 10 September 1800 to her childhood friend, Jane Pollard (Mrs John Marshall):

> We are daily more delighted with Grasmere, and its neighbourhood; our walks are perpetually varied, and we are more fond of the mountains as our acquaintance with them increases. We have a boat upon the lake and a small orchard and a smaller *garden* which as it is the work of our own hands we regard with pride and partiality. This garden we enclosed from the road and pulled down a fence which formerly divided it from the orchard. The orchard is very small, but then it is a delightful one from its retirement, and the

excessive beauty of the prospect from it. Our cottage is quite large enough for us though very small, and we have made it neat and comfortable within doors and it looks very nice on the outside, for though the roses and honeysuckles which we have planted against it are only of this year's growth yet it is covered all over with green leaves and scarlet flowers, for we have trained scarlet beans upon threads, which are not only exceedingly beautiful, but very useful, as their produce is immense. The only objection we have to our house is that it is rather too near the road, and from its smallness and the manner in which it is built noises pass from one part of the house to the other, so that if we had any visitors a sick person could not be in quietness. We have made a lodging room of the parlour below stairs, which has a stone floor therefore we have covered it all over with matting. The bed, though only a camp bed, is large enough for two people to sleep in. We sit in a room above stairs and we have one lodging room with two single beds, a sort of lumber room and a small low unceiled room, which I have papered with newspapers and in which we have put a small bed without curtains.

JONATHAN WORDSWORTH

Oxford, 1987

A Note on the Text

The text of this edition has been newly prepared by Pamela Woof, Lecturer in Literature, Centre of Continuing Education, University of Newcastle, from the original journals in the Wordsworth Library, Dove Cottage, and incorporates many new readings, but it is not intended as an exact transcription. Mistakes in dating have been silently corrected, and the date headings regularised. Spelling has been modernised and made consistent, although some unusual spellings of names and places have been retained where these would cause no difficulty (e.g. Rydale, not Rydal). Punctuation has been very sparingly amended where the sense was unclear, and the use of capitals has been modernised. At a handful of points, unreadable words or part-sentences have been silently deleted. Gaps in the chronology are caused sometimes by Dorothy Wordsworth neglecting to write for a while, and sometimes by missing pages. There is a major gap between 22 December 1800 and 9 October 1801 where a whole notebook has been lost.

A Note on the Illustrations

Picture credits and an index of artists can be found on page 188. All uncaptioned decorations in the text are wood engravings by Thomas Bewick. The cloud study marking year breaks is by John Constable. The map is specially drawn by John Mitchell.

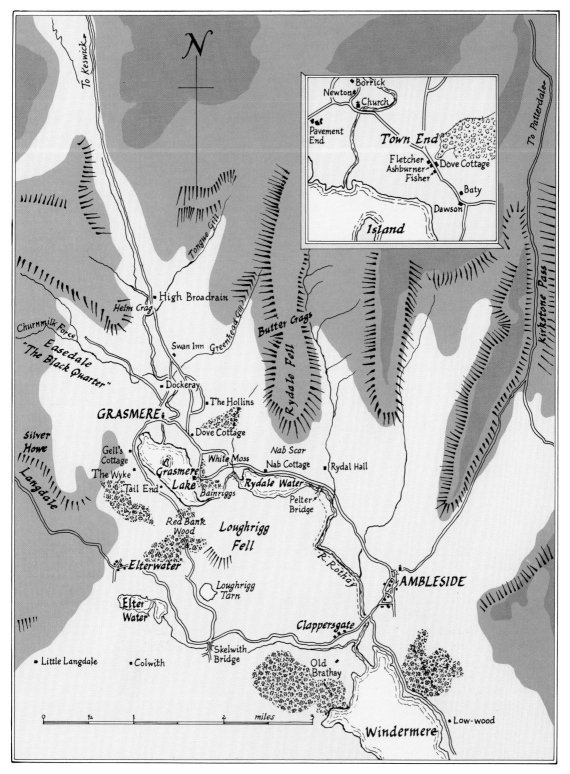

N

To Keswick

To Patterdale

Town End

Borrick
Newton
Church
Pavement
End
Fletcher
Ashburner
Fisher
Dove Cottage
Baty
Dawson
Island

Kirkstone Pass

Tongue Gill

Churnmilk Force

Helm Crag

High Broadrain

Easedale
"The Black Quarter"

Swan Inn

Greenhead Gill

Butter Crags

Rydale Fell

Dockeray

The Hollins

GRASMERE

Dove Cottage

Silver
Howe

Gell's
Cottage

Nab Scar

White Moss

Nab Cottage

Rydal Hall

The Wyke

**Grasmere
Lake**

Langdale

Tail End

Bainriggs

Rydale Water

Pelter
Bridge

Red Bank
Wood

**Loughrigg
Fell**

R. Rothay

AMBLESIDE

Elterwater

Loughrigg
Tarn

Elter
Water

Clappersgate

Little Langdale

Colwith

Skelwith
Bridge

Old
Brathay

Low-wood

0   ½   1   2   miles   3

Windermere

Dorothy Wordsworth's Grasmere

· *1800* ·

Wednesday 14 May

Wm and John set off into Yorkshire after dinner at half past two o'clock, cold pork in their pockets. I left them at the turning of the Low-wood bay under the trees. My heart was so full that I could hardly speak to W. when I gave him a farewell kiss. I sat a long time upon a stone at the margin of the lake, and after a flood of tears my heart was easier. The lake looked to me I knew not why dull and melancholy, and the weltering on the shores seemed a heavy sound. I walked as long as I could amongst the stones of the shore. The wood rich in flowers. A beautiful yellow, palish yellow flower, that looked thick round and double, and smelt very sweet—I supposed it was a ranunculus—crowfoot, the grassy-leaved rabbit-toothed white flower, strawberries, geranium—scentless violet, anemones two kinds, orchises, primroses. The heckberry very beautiful, the crab coming out as a low shrub. Met a blind man, driving a very large beautiful bull and a cow—he walked with two sticks. Came home by Clappersgate. The valley very green, many sweet views up to Rydale head when I could juggle away the fine houses, but they disturbed me even more than when I have been happier. One beautiful view of the bridge, without Sir Michael's. Sat down very often, though it was cold. I resolved to write a journal of the time till W. and J. return, and I set about keeping my resolve because I will not quarrel with myself, and because I shall give Wm pleasure by it when he comes home again. At Rydale a woman of the village, stout and well dressed, begged a halfpenny—she had never she said done it before, but these hard times— —Arrived at home with a bad headache, set some slips of privet. The evening cold, had a fire—my face now flame-coloured. It is nine o'clock. I shall soon go to bed. A young woman begged at the door—she had come from Manchester on Sunday morn with two shillings and a slip of paper which she supposed a bank note—it was a cheat. She had buried her husband and three children within a year and a half—all in one grave—burying very dear—paupers all put in one place—twenty shillings paid for as much ground as will bury a man—a gravestone to be put over it or the right will be lost—eleven shillings and sixpence each time the ground is opened. Oh! that I had a letter from William.

Thursday 15 May

A coldish dull morning—hoed the first row of peas, weeded etc. etc., sat hard to mending till evening and the rain which had threatened all day came on just when I was going to walk.

Friday 16 May

Warm and mild, after a fine night of rain. Transplanted radishes after breakfast, walked to Mr Gell's with the books, gathered mosses and plants. The woods extremely beautiful with all autumnal variety and softness. I carried a basket for mosses, and gathered some wild plants. Oh! that we had a book of botany. All flowers now are gay and deliciously sweet. The primrose still pre-eminent among the later flowers of the spring. Foxgloves very tall, with their heads budding. I went forward round the lake at the foot of Loughrigg fell. I was much amused with the business of a pair of stone chats. Their restless voices as they skimmed along the water following each other their shadows under them, and their returning back to the stones on the shore, chirping with the same unwearied voice. Could not cross the water so I went round by the stepping stones. The morning clear but cloudy, that is the hills were not overhung by mists. After dinner

Aggy weeded onions and carrots. I helped for a little—wrote to Mary Hutchinson—washed my head—worked. After tea went to Ambleside— a pleasant cool but not cold evening. Rydale was very beautiful with spear-shaped streaks of polished steel. No letters!—only one newspaper. I returned by Clappersgate. Grasmere was very solemn in the last glimpse of twilight it calls home the heart to quietness. I had been very melancholy in my walk back. I had many of my saddest thoughts and I could not keep the tears within me. But when I came to Grasmere I felt that it did me good. I finished my letter to M. H. Ate hasty pudding, and went to bed. As I was going out in the morning I met a half-crazy old man. He showed me a pincushion and begged a pin, afterwards a halfpenny. He began in a kind of indistinct voice in this manner: 'Matthew Jobson's lost a cow. Tom Nichol has two good horses strained. Jim Jones's cow's brokken her horn, etc. etc.' He went into Aggy's and persuaded her to give him some whey and let him boil some porridge. She declares he ate two quarts.

Saturday 17 May

Incessant rain from morning till night. T. Ashburner brought us coals. Worked hard and read *Midsummer Night's Dream, Ballads*—sauntered a little in the garden. The skobby sat quietly in its nest rocked by the winds and beaten by the rain.

skobby: chaffinch

Sunday 18 May

Went to church, slight showers, a cold air. The mountains from this window look much greener and I think the valley is more green than ever. The corn begins to show itself. The ashes are still bare. Went part of the way home with Miss Simpson. A little girl from Coniston came to beg. She had lain out all night—her step-mother had turned her out of doors. Her father could not stay at home, 'She flights so'. Walked to Ambleside in the evening round the lake. The prospect exceedingly beautiful from Loughrigg fell. It was so green, that no eye could be weary of reposing upon it. The most beautiful situation for

Grasmere from Loughrigg Fell, by George Pickering

The road outside Dove Cottage, by T. M. Richardson.
To the left are Ashburner's and Fletcher the carrier's

a house in the field next to Mr Benson's. It threatened rain all the evening but was mild and pleasant. I was overtaken by two Cumberland people on the other side of Rydale who complimented me upon my walking. They were going to sell cloth, and odd things which they make themselves in Hawkshead and the neighbourhood. The post was not arrived so I walked through the town, past Mrs Taylor's, and met him. Letters from Coleridge and Cottle. John Fisher overtook me on the other side of Rydale. He talked much about the alteration in the times, and observed that in a short time there would be only two ranks of people, the very rich and the very poor, for those who have small estates says he are forced to sell, and all the land goes into one hand. Did not reach home till ten o'clock.

Monday 19 May

Sauntered a good deal in the garden, bound carpets, mended old clothes. Read *Timon of Athens*. Dried linen. Molly weeded the turnips. John stuck the peas. We had not much sunshine or wind but no rain till about seven o'clock when we had a slight shower just after I had set out upon my walk. I did not return but walked up into the Black Quarter. I sauntered a long time among the rocks above the church. The most delightful situation possible for a cottage commanding two distinct views of the vale and of the lake, is among those rocks. I strolled on, gathered mosses, etc. The quietness and still seclusion of the valley affected me even to producing the deepest melancholy. I forced myself from it.

The wind rose before I went to bed. No rain—Dodwell and Wilkinson called in my absence.

Tuesday 20 May

A fine mild rain. After breakfast the sky cleared and before the clouds passed from the hill, I went to Ambleside. It was a sweet morning. Everything green and over-flowing with life, and the streams making a perpetual song with the thrushes and all little birds, not forgetting the stone chats. The post was not come in. I walked as far as Windermere, and met him there. No letters! no papers. Came home by Clappersgate. I was sadly tired, ate a hasty dinner and had a bad headache. Went to bed and slept at least two hours. Rain came on in the evening—Molly washing.

Wednesday 21 May

Went often to spread the linen which was bleaching—a rainy day and very wet night.

Thursday 22 May

A very fine day with showers—dried the linen and starched. Drank tea at Mr Simpson's. Brought down batchelor's buttons (rock ranunculus) and other plants—went part of the way back. A showery, mild evening—all the peas up.

Friday 23 May

Ironing till tea time. So heavy a rain that I could not go for letters—put by the linen, mended stockings etc.

Saturday 24 May

Walked in the morning to Ambleside. I found a letter from Wm and from Mary Hutchinson and Douglass. Returned on the other side of the lakes—wrote to William after dinner, nailed up the beds, worked in the garden, sat in the evening under the trees. I went to bed soon with a bad headache. A fine day.

Sunday 25 May

A very fine warm day, had no fire. Read *Macbeth* in the morning, sat under the trees after dinner. Miss Simpson came just as I was going out and she sat with me. I wrote to my brother Christopher, and sent John Fisher to Ambleside after tea. Miss Simpson and I walked to the foot of the lake—her brother met us. I went with them nearly home and on my return found a letter from Coleridge and from Charles Lloyd, and three papers.

Monday 26 May

A very fine morning, worked in the garden till after ten when old Mr Simpson came and talked to me till after twelve. Molly weeding. Wrote letters to J. H., Coleridge, C. Ll., and W. I walked towards Rydale and turned aside at my favourite field. The air and the lake were still—one cottage light in the vale, and so much of the day left that I could distinguish objects, the woods; trees and houses. Two or three different kinds of birds sang at intervals on the opposite shore. I sat till I could hardly drag myself away I grew so sad. 'When pleasant thoughts,' etc. . . . .

Tuesday 27 May

I walked to Ambleside with letters—met the post before I reached Mr Partridge's, one paper, only a letter for Coleridge—I expected a letter from Wm. It was a sweet morning, the ashes in the valleys nearly in full leaf but still to be distinguished, quite bare on the higher grounds. I was warm on returning, and becoming cold with sitting in the house— I had a bad headache—went to bed after dinner, and lay till after five—not well after tea. I worked in the garden, but did not walk further. A delightful evening before the sun set but afterwards it grew colder. Mended stockings etc.

Above Grasmere, by John Harden

Wednesday 28 May

In the morning walked up to the rocks above Jenny Dockeray's sat a long time upon the grass the prospect divinely beautiful. If I had three hundred pounds and could afford to have a bad interest for my money I would buy that estate, and we would build a cottage there to end our days in. I went into her garden and got white and yellow lilies, periwinkle, etc., which I planted. Sat under the trees with my work. No fire in the morning. Worked till between seven and eight, and then watered the garden, and was about to go up to Mr Simpson's, when Miss S. and her visitors passed the door. I went home with them, a beautiful evening the crescent moon hanging above Helm Crag.

Thursday 29 May

In the morning worked in the garden a little, read *King John*. Miss Simpson, and Miss Falcon and Mr S. came very early. Went to Mr Gell's boat before tea. We fished upon the lake and amongst us caught thirteen bass. Miss Simpson brought gooseberries *and cream*. Left the water at near nine o'clock, very cold. Went part of the way home with the party.

Friday 30 May

In the morning went to Ambleside, forgetting that the post does not come till the evening. How was I grieved when I was so informed. I walked back resolving to go again in the evening. It rained very mildly and sweetly in the morning as I came home, but came on a wet afternoon and evening—but chilly. I caught Mr Olliff's lad as he was going for letters, he brought me one from Wm and twelve papers. I planted London pride upon the well and many things on the borders. John sodded the well. As I came past Rydale in the morning I saw a heron swimming with only its neck out of water—it beat and struggled amongst the water when it flew away and was long in getting loose.

Saturday 31 May

A sweet mild rainy morning. Grundy the carpet man called. I paid him one pound ten shillings. Went to the blind man's for plants. I got such a load that I was obliged to leave my basket in the road and send Molly for it. Planted. After dinner when I was putting up vallances Miss Simpson and her visitors called. I went with them to Brathay Bridge. We got broom in returning, strawberries, etc., came home by Ambleside. Grasmere looked divinely beautiful. Mr, Miss Simpson and Tommy drank tea at eight o'clock. I walked to the potter's with them.

Sunday 1 June

Rain in the night—a sweet mild morning. Read *Ballads*; went to church. Singers from Wytheburn. Went part of the way home with Miss Simpson. Walked upon the hill above the house till dinner time—went again to church—a christening and singing which kept us very late. The pew-side came down with me. Walked with Miss Simpson nearly home. After tea went to Ambleside, round the lakes—a very fine warm evening. I lay upon the steep of Loughrigg my heart dissolved in what I saw when I was not startled but recalled from my reverie by a noise as of a child paddling without shoes. I looked up and saw a lamb close to me. It approached nearer and nearer as if to examine me and stood a

Brathay Bridge, by John Harden

long time. I did not move. At last it ran past me and went bleating along the pathway seeming to be seeking its mother. I saw a hare in the high road. The post was not come in; I waited in the road till John's apprentice came with a letter from Coleridge and three papers. The moon shone upon the water—reached home at ten o'clock—went to bed immediately. Molly brought daisies etc. which we planted.

Monday 2 June

A cold dry windy morning. I worked in the garden and planted flowers, etc. Sat under the trees after dinner till tea time. John Fisher stuck the peas, Molly weeded and washed. I went to Ambleside after tea, crossed the stepping stones at the foot of Grasmere and pursued my way on the other side of Rydale and by Clappersgate. I sat a long time to watch the hurrying waves and to hear the regularly irregular sound of the dashing waters. The waves round about the little island seemed like a dance of spirits that rose out of the water, round its small circumference of shore. Inquired about lodgings for Coleridge, and was accompanied by Mrs Nicholson as far as Rydale. This was very kind, but God be thanked I want not society by a moonlight lake—It was near eleven when I reached home. I wrote to Coleridge and went late to bed.

Tuesday 3 June

Sent off my letter by the butcher—a boisterous drying day. Worked in the garden before dinner. Read *Richard II*—was not well after dinner and lay down. Mrs Simpson's grandson brought me some gooseberries. I got up and walked with him part of the way home, afterwards went down rambling by the lakeside—got lockety goldings, strawberries etc., and planted. After tea the wind fell. I walked towards Mr Simpson's. Gave the newpapers to the girl, reached home at ten. No letter, no William—a letter from Rd to John.

Wednesday 4 June

A very fine day. I sat out of doors most of the day, wrote to Mr Jackson. Ambleside fair. I walked to the lakeside in the morning, took up plants and sat upon a stone reading *Ballads*. In the evening I was watering plants when Mr and Miss Simpson called. I accompanied them home, and we went to the waterfall at the head of the valley. It was very interesting in the twilight. I brought home lemon thyme and several other plants, and planted them by moonlight. I lingered out of doors in the hope of hearing my brother's tread.

Thursday 5 June

thrid: thread

I sat out of doors great part of the day and worked in the garden—had a letter from Mr Jackson, and wrote an answer to Coleridge. The little birds busy making love and pecking the blossoms bits of moss off the trees, they flutter about and about and thrid the trees as I lie under them. Molly went out to tea, I would not go far from home, expecting my brothers. I rambled on the hill above the house gathered wild thyme and took up roots of wild columbine. Just as I was returning with my 'load', Mr and Miss Simpson called. We went again upon the hill, got more plants, set them, and then went to the blind man's for London pride for Miss Simpson. I went up with them as far as the blacksmith's. A fine lovely moonlight night.

Mountain scene, by John Constable

Friday 6 June

Sat out of doors reading the whole afternoon, but in the morning I wrote to my aunt Cookson. In the evening I went to Ambleside with Coleridge's letter—it was a lovely night as the day had been. I went by Loughrigg and Clappersgate and just met the post at the turnpike—he told me there were two letters but none for me. So I was in no hurry and went round again by Clappersgate, crossed the stepping stones and entered Ambleside at Matthew Harrison's. A letter from Jack Hutchinson, and one from Montagu enclosing a three pound note. No William! I slackened my pace as I came near home fearing to hear that he was not come. I listened till after one o'clock to every barking dog, cock fighting, and other sports: it was Mr Borrick's opening. Foxgloves just coming into blossom.

Saturday 7 June

A very warm cloudy morning, threatening to rain. I walked up to Mr Simpson's to gather gooseberries—it was a very fine afternoon. Little Tommy came down with me, ate gooseberry pudding and drank tea with me. We went up the hill to gather sods and plants and went down to the lakeside and took up orchises etc. I watered the garden and weeded. I did not leave home in the expectation of Wm and John, and sitting at work till after eleven o'clock I heard a foot go to the front of the house, turn round, and open the gate. It was William— —After our first joy was over, we got some tea. We did not go to bed till four o'clock in the morning so he had an opportunity of seeing our improvements. The birds were singing and all looked fresh, though not gay. There was a greyness on earth and sky. We did not rise till near ten in the morning. We were busy all day in writing letters to Coleridge, Montagu, Douglass, Richard. Mr and Miss Simpson called in the evening, the little boy carried our letters to Ambleside. We walked with Mr and Miss S. home on their return. The evening was cold and I was afraid of the toothache for William. We met John on our return home.

Monday 9 June

In the morning W. cut down the winter cherry tree. I sowed French beans and weeded. A coronetted landau went by when we were sitting upon the sodded wall. The ladies (evidently tourists) turned an eye of interest upon our little garden and cottage. We went to R. Newton's for pike floats and went round to Mr Gell's boat and on to the lake to fish. We caught nothing—it was extremely cold. The reeds and bulrushes or bullpipes of a tender soft green, making a plain whose surface moved with the wind. The reeds not yet tall. The lake clear to the bottom, but saw no fish. In the evening I stuck peas, watered the garden and planted broccoli. Did not walk for it was very cold. A poor girl called to beg who had no work at home and was going in search of it to Kendal. She slept in Mr Benson's lathe, and went off after breakfast in the morning with sevenpence and a letter to the mayor of Kendal.

Tuesday 10 June

A cold, yet sunshiny morning. John carried letters to Ambleside. I made tarts, pies etc. Wm stuck peas. After dinner he lay down. John not at home. I stuck peas alone. Molly washing. Cold showers with hail and rain, but at half-past five after a heavy rain the lake became calm—and very beautiful. Those parts of the water which were perfectly unruffled lay like green islands of various shapes. W. and I walked to Ambleside to seek lodgings for C. No letters. No papers. It was a very cold cheerless evening. John had been fishing in Langdale and was gone to bed.

On Tuesday, May 27th, a very tall woman, tall much beyond the measure of tall women, called at the door. She had on a very long brown cloak, and a very white cap without bonnet—her face was excessively brown, but it had plainly once been fair. She led a little bare-footed child about two years old by the hand and said her husband who was a tinker was gone before with the other children. I gave her a piece of bread. Afterwards on my road to Ambleside, beside the bridge at Rydale, I saw her husband sitting by the roadside, his two asses feeding beside him and the two young children at play upon the grass. The man did not beg. I passed on and about a quarter of a mile further I saw two boys before me, one about ten the other about eight years old at play chasing a butterfly. They were wild figures, not very ragged, but without shoes and stockings; the hat of the elder was wreathed round with yellow flowers, the younger whose hat was only a rimless crown, had stuck it round with laurel leaves. They continued at play till I drew very near and then they addressed me with the beggars' cant and the whining voice of sorrow. I said I served your mother this morning. (The boys were so like the woman who had called at the door that I could not be mistaken.) O! says the elder you could not serve my mother for she's dead and my father's on at the next town—he's a potter. I persisted in my assertion and that I would give them nothing. Says the elder Come, let's away, and away they flew like lightning. They had however sauntered so long in their road that they did not reach Ambleside before me, and I saw them go up to Matthew Harrison's house with their wallet upon the elder's shoulder, and creeping with a beggar's complaining foot. On my return through Ambleside I met in the street the mother driving her asses; in the two panniers of one of which were the two

Beggars, by Gavarni

little children whom she was chiding and threatening with a wand which she used to drive on her asses, while the little things hung in wantonness over the pannier's edge. The woman had told me in the morning that she was of Scotland, which her accent fully proved, but that she had lived I think at Wigton, that they could not keep a house and so they travelled.

Wednesday 11 June

A very cold morning—we went on the lake to set pike floats with John's fish. W. and J. went first alone. Mr Simpson called, and I accompanied him to the lakeside. My brothers and I again went upon the water, and returned to dinner. We landed upon the island where I saw the whitest hawthorn I have seen this year, the generality of hawthorns are bloomless. I saw wild roses in the hedges. Went to bed in the afternoon and slept till after six—a threatening of the toothache. Wm and John went to the pike floats—they brought in two pikes. I sowed kidney-beans and spinach. A cold evening. Molly stuck the peas. I weeded a little. Did not walk.

Thursday 12 June

William and I went upon the water to set pike floats. John fished under Loughrigg. We returned to dinner, two pikes boiled and roasted. Very cold air but warm sun. W. and I again went upon the water. We walked to Rydale after tea, and up to the potter's. A cold night, but warmer.

Friday 13 June

A rainy morning. W. and J. went upon the lake. Very warm, and pleasant gleams of sunshine. Went upon the water after tea, caught a pike seven and a half lbs. Mr Simpson trolling. Mr Gell and his party came.

Saturday 14 June

A fine morning but cloudy. W. and John went upon the lake. I stayed at home. We drank tea at Mr Simpson's. Stayed till after ten o'clock.

Sunday 15 June

John walked to Coniston. W. and I sauntered in the garden. Afterwards walked by the lakeside: a cold air. We pushed through the wood. Walked behind the fir grove and returned to dinner. We lay down after dinner. Parker, the tanner and the blacksmith from Hawkshead called.

Monday 16 June

Wm and I went to Brathay by Little Langdale and Collath and Skelleth. It was a warm mild morning with threatening of rain. The vale of Little Langdale looked bare and unlovely. Collath was wild and interesting, from the peat carts and peat gatherers—the valley all perfumed with the gale and wild thyme. The woods about the waterfall veined with rich yellow broom. A succession of delicious views from Skelleth to Brathay. We met near Skelleth a pretty little boy with a wallet over his shoulder—he came from Hawkshead and was going to 'late' a lock of meal. He spoke gently and without

'late' a lock of meal: search for some meal

View from Brathay, by John Harden

complaint. When I asked him if he got enough to eat he looked surprised and said 'Nay'. He was seven years old but seemed not more than five. We drank tea at Mr Ibbetson's, and returned by Ambleside. Lent three pounds nine shillings to the potter at Kendal. Met John on our return home at about ten o'clock. Saw a primrose in blossom.

Tuesday 17 June

We put the new window in. I ironed and worked about a good deal in house and garden. In the evening we walked for letters. Found one for Coleridge at Rydale, and I returned much tired.

Wednesday 18 June

We walked round the lake in the morning and in the evening to the lower waterfall at Rydale. It was a warm dark, lowering evening.

Thursday 19 June

A very hot morning. W. and I walked up to Mr Simpson's. W. and old Mr S. went to fish in Wytheburn water. I dined with John, and lay under the trees. The afternoon changed from clear to cloudy and to clear again. John and I walked up to the waterfall and to Mr Simpson's, and with Miss Simpson met the fishers. W. caught a pike weighing four and three quarter lbs. There was a gloom almost terrible over Grasmere water and vale. A few drops fell but not much rain. No Coleridge whom we fully expected.

Friday 20 June

I worked in the garden in the morning. Wm prepared pea sticks. Threatening for rain but

Eller Water

yet it comes not. On Wednesday evening a poor man called, a hatter—he had been long ill, but was now recovered and his wife was lying in of her fourth child. The parish would not help him because he had implements of trade etc. etc. We gave him sixpence.

Saturday 21 June

In the morning W. and I went to Ambleside to get his tooth drawn, and put in. A fine clear morning but cold. W.'s tooth drawn with very little pain—he slept till three o'clock. Young Mr S. drank tea and supped with us then fished in Rydale water and they caught two small fishes—W. no bite—John three. Miss Simpson and three children called—I walked with them to Rydale. The evening cold and clear and frosty, but the wind was falling as I returned. I stayed at home about an hour and then walked up the hill to Rydale lake. Grasmere looked so beautiful that my heart was almost melted away. It was quite calm only spotted with sparkles of light. The church visible. On our return all distant objects had faded away—all but the hills. The reflection of the light bright sky above Black Quarter was very solemn. Mr S. did not go till twelve o'clock.

Sunday 22 June

In the morning W. and I walked towards Rydale and up into the wood but finding it not

Elterwater, by Francis Towne

very pleasant we returned—sauntered in the garden—a showery day. In the evening I planted a honeysuckle round the yew tree. In the evening we walked for letters. No letters: no news of Coleridge. Jimmy Benson came home drunk beside us.

Monday 23 June

Mr Simpson called in the morning. Tommy's father dead. W. and I went into Langdale to fish. The morning was very cold. I sat at the foot of the lake till my head ached with cold. The view exquisitely beautiful, through a gate and under a sycamore tree beside the first house going into Loughrigg. Elterwater looked barren, and the view from the church less beautiful than in winter. When W. went down to the water to fish I lay under the wind my head pillowed upon a mossy rock and slept about ten minutes, which relieved my headache. We ate our dinner together and parted again. Wm was afraid he had lost his line and sought me. An old man saw me just after I had crossed the stepping stones and was going through a copse—Ho, where were you going? To Elterwater Bridge— Why says he it's well I saw you ye were gane to Little Langdale by Wrynose, and several other places, which he ran over with a mixture of triumph, good-nature, and wit—It's well I saw you or you'd ha' been lost. The evening grew very pleasant—we sat on the side of the hill looking to Elterwater. I was much tired and returned home to tea. W. went to fish for pike in Rydale. John came in when I had done tea, and he and I carried a jug of tea to William. We met him in the old road from Rydale. He drank his tea upon the turf. The setting sun threw a red purple light upon the rocks and stone walls of Rydale which gave them a most interesting and beautiful appearance.

Tuesday 24 June

W. went to Ambleside. John walked out. I made tarts etc. Mr B. Simpson called and asked us to tea. I went to the view of Rydale to meet William. John went to him—I returned. W. and I drank tea at Mr Simpson's. Brought down lemon thyme, greens etc. The old woman was very happy to see us and we were so in the pleasure we gave. She was an affecting picture of patient disappointment, suffering under no particular affliction.

Wednesday 25 June

A very rainy day. I made a shoe. Wm and John went to fish in Langdale. In the evening I went above the house, and gathered flowers which I planted, foxgloves, etc.

The head of Windermere, by John Harden

On Sunday Mr and Mrs Coleridge and Hartley came. The day was very warm. We sailed to the foot of Loughrigg. They stayed with us three weeks and till the Thursday following, i.e. till the 24th of July. On the Friday preceding their departure we drank tea at the island. The weather very delightful, and on the Sunday we made a great fire, and drank tea in Bainriggs with the Simpsons. I accompanied Mrs C. to Wytheburn, and returned with W.—to tea at Mr Simpson's—it was excessively hot, but the day after Friday July 25th still hotter. All the morning I was engaged in unpacking our Somersetshire goods and in making pies. The house was a hot oven but yet we could not bake the pies. I was so weary I could not walk, so I went and sat with Wm in the orchard. We had a delightful half hour in the warm still evening.

Saturday 26 July

Still hotter. I sat with W. in the orchard all the morning and made my shoe. In the afternoon from excessive heat I was ill in the headache and toothache and went to bed—I was refreshed with washing myself after I got up, but it was too hot to walk till near dark, and then I sat upon the wall finishing my shoes.

Sunday 27 July

Very warm. Molly ill. John bathed in the lake. I wrote out 'Ruth' in the afternoon, in the morning I read ·Mr Knight's *Landscape*. After tea we rowed down to Loughrigg Fell, visited the white foxglove, gathered wild strawberries, and walked up to view Rydale. We lay a long time looking at the lake, the shores all embrowned with the scorching sun. The ferns were turning yellow, that is here and there one was quite turned. We walked round by Benson's wood home. The lake was now most still and reflected the beautiful yellow and blue and purple and grey colours of the sky. We heard a strange sound in the Bainriggs wood as we were floating on the water it *seemed* in the wood, but it must have

been above it, for presently we saw a raven very high above us—it called out and the dome of the sky seemed to echo the sound—it called again and again as it flew onwards, and the mountains gave back the sound, seeming as if from their centre a musical bell-like answering to the bird's hoarse voice. We heard both the call of the bird and the echo after we could see him no longer. We walked up to the top of the hill again in view of Rydale. Met Mr and Miss Simpson on horseback. The crescent moon which had shone upon the water was now gone down. Returned to supper at ten o'clock.

Monday 28 July

Received a letter from Coleridge enclosing one from Mr Davy about the *Lyrical Ballads*. Intensely hot. I made pies in the morning. Wm went into the wood and altered his poems. In the evening it was so very warm that I was too much tired to walk.

Tuesday 29 July

Still very hot. We gathered peas for dinner. We walked up in the evening to find out Hewetson's cottage but it was too dark. I was sick and weary.

Buttermere Lake, by J. M. W. Turner

Wednesday 30 July

Gathered peas for Mrs Simpson—John and I walked up with them—very hot—Wm had intended going to Keswick. I was obliged to lie down after dinner from excessive heat and headache. The evening excessively beautiful—a rich reflection of the moon, the moonlight clouds and the hills, and from the Rays gap a huge rainbow pillar. We sailed upon the lake till it was ten o'clock.

Thursday 31 July

All the morning I was busy copying poems. Gathered peas, and in the afternoon Coleridge came, very hot, he brought the second volume of the *Anthology*. The men went to bathe, and we afterwards sailed down to Loughrigg. Read poems on the water, and let the boat take its own course. We walked a long time upon Loughrigg and returned in the grey twilight. The moon just setting as we reached home.

Friday 1 August

In the morning I copied 'The Brothers'. Coleridge and Wm went down to the lake. They returned and we all went together to Mary Point where we sat in the breeze and the shade, and read Wm's poems. Altered 'The Whirlblast' etc. Mr Simpson came to tea and Mr B. Simpson afterwards. We drank tea in the orchard.

Saturday 2 August

Wm and Coleridge went to Keswick. John went with them to Wytheburn and stayed all day fishing and brought home two small pikes at night. I accompanied them to Lewthwaite's cottage and on my return papered Wm's room. I afterwards lay down till tea time and after tea worked at my shifts in the orchard. A grey evening. About eight o'clock it gathered for rain and I had the scatterings of a shower, but afterwards the lake became of a glassy calmness and all was still. I sat till I could see no longer and then continued my work in the house.

Sunday 3 August

I made pies and stuffed the pike—baked a loaf. Headache after dinner—I lay down. A letter from Wm roused me, desiring us to go to Keswick. After writing to Wm we walked as far as Mr Simpson's and ate black cherries. A heavenly warm evening with scattered clouds upon the hills. There was a vernal greenness upon the grass from the rains of the morning and afternoon. Peas for dinner.

Monday 4 August

Rain in the night. I tied up scarlet beans, nailed the honeysuckles etc. etc. John was prepared to walk to Keswick all the morning. He seized a returned chaise and went after dinner. I pulled a large basket of peas and sent to Keswick by a returned chaise. A very cold evening. Assisted to spread out linen in the morning.

Tuesday 5 August

Dried the linen in the morning, the air still cold. I pulled a bag full of peas for Mrs Simpson. Miss Simpson drank tea with me and supped on her return from Ambleside. A very fine evening. I sat on the wall making my shifts till I could see no longer. Walked half-way home with Miss Simpson.

Wednesday 6 August

A rainy morning. I ironed till dinner time—sewed till near dark—then pulled a basket of peas, and afterwards boiled and picked gooseberries. William came home from Keswick at eleven o'clock. A very fine night.

Thursday 7 August

Packed up the mattress, and sent to Keswick. Boiled gooseberries—N.B. 2 lbs of sugar in the first panful, 3 quarts all good measure—3 lbs in the second, 4 quarts—2½ lbs in the third. A very fine day. William composing in the wood in the morning. In the evening we walked to Mary Point. A very fine sunset.

Friday 8 August

We intended going to Keswick, but were prevented by the excessive heat. Nailed up scarlet beans in the morning. Drank tea at Mr Simpson's, and walked over the mountains by Wattenlath. Very fine gooseberries at Mr S.'s A most enchanting walk. Wattenlath a heavenly scene. Reached Coleridge's at eleven o'clock.

Saturday 9 August

I walked with Coleridge in the Windy Brow woods.

Sunday 10 August

Very hot. The C.s went to church. We sailed upon Derwent in the evening.

Monday 11 August

Walked to Windy Brow.

Tuesday 12 August

Drank tea with the Cockins—Wm and I walked along the Cockermouth road. He was altering his poems.

Wednesday 13 August

Made the Windy Brow seat.

Thursday 14 August

Called at the Speddings. In the evening walked in the wood with W. Very very beautiful the moon.

Study at Rydale, by William Green

Friday 15 August

W. in the wood—I went with Hartley to see the Cockins and to buy bacon. In the evening we walked to Water End—feasted on gooseberries at Silver Hill.

Saturday 16 August

Worked for Mrs C.—and walked with Coleridge intending to gather raspberries—joined by Miss Spedding.

Sunday 17 August

Came home. Dined in Borrowdale. A rainy morning but a fine evening—saw the Bristol prison and Bassenthwaite at the same time—Wm read us 'The Seven Sisters' on a stone.

Derwentwater, by Edward Dayes

Monday 18 August

Putting linen by and mending. Walked with John to Mr Simpson's and met Wm in returning. A fine warm day.

Tuesday 19 August

Mr and Mrs Simpson dined with us—Miss S. and brother drank tea in the orchard.

Wednesday 20 August

I worked in the morning. Cold in the evening and rainy. Did not walk.

Thursday 21 August

Read Wallenstein and sent it off—worked in the morning—walked with John round the two lakes—gathered white foxglove seeds and found Wm in Bainriggs at our return.

Friday 22 August

Very cold. Baking in the morning, gathered pea seeds and took up—lighted a fire upstairs. Walked as far as Rydale with John intending to have gone on to Ambleside but we found the papers at Rydale—Wm walking in the wood all the time. John and he went out after our return—I mended stockings. Wind very high shaking the corn.

Saturday 23 August

A very fine morning. Wm was composing all the morning. I shelled peas, gathered beans, and worked in the garden till half past twelve then walked with William in the wood. The gleams of sunshine and the stirring trees and gleaming bright, cheerful lake, most delightful. After dinner we walked to Ambleside—showery—went to see Mr

Partridge's house. Came home by Clappersgate. We had intended going by Rydale woods, but it was cold—I was not well, and tired. Got tea immediately and had a fire. Did not reach home till seven o'clock—mended stockings—and W. read 'Peter Bell'. He read us the poem of 'Joanna' beside the Rothay by the roadside.

Sunday 24 August

A fine cool pleasant breezy day—walked in the wood in the morning. Mr Twining called. John walked up to Mr Simpson's in the evening. I stayed at home and wrote to Mrs Rawson and my aunt Cookson—I was ill in the afternoon and lay down—got up restored by a sound sleep.

Monday 25 August

A fine day—walked in the wood in the morning and to the fir grove—walked up to Mr Simpson's in the evening.

Tuesday 26 August

We walked in the evening to Ambleside. Wm not quite well. I bought sacking for the mattress. A very fine solemn evening. The wind blew very free from the island and at Rydale. We went on the other side of Rydale, and sat a long time looking at the mountains, which were all black at Grasmere and very bright in Rydale—Grasmere exceedingly dark and Rydale of a light yellow green.

Wednesday 27 August

In the morning we walked. John Baty passed us. We walked along the shore of the lake in the evening, and went over into Langdale and down to Loughrigg Tarn—a very fine evening calm and still.

Thursday 28 August

Still very fine weather. I baked bread and cakes. In the evening we walked round the lake by Rydale. Mr Simpson came to fish.

Friday 29 August

We walked to Rydale to inquire for letters. We walked over the hill by the fir grove. I sat upon a rock and observed a flight of swallows gathering together high above my head they flew towards Rydale. We walked through the wood over the stepping stones. The lake of Rydale very beautiful, partly still. John and I left Wm to compose an inscription—that about the path. We had a very fine walk by the gloomy lake. There was a curious yellow reflection in the water as of cornfields. There was no light in the clouds from which it appeared to come.

Saturday 30 August

I was baking bread, pies and dinner. It was very warm. Wm finished his inscription of the pathway, then walked in the wood and when John returned he sought him and they bathed together. I read a little of Boswell's *Life of Johnson*. I had a headache and went to lie down in the orchard. I was roused by a shout that Anthony Harrison was come. We sat in the orchard till tea time, drank tea early and rowed down the lake which was stirred by breezes. We looked at Rydale which was soft, cheerful, and beautiful. We then went to peep into Langdale. The Pikes were very grand. We walked back to the view of Rydale, which was now a dark mirror. We rowed home over a lake still as glass and then went to George Mackareth's to hire a horse for John. A fine moonlight night. The beauty of the moon was startling as it rose to us over Loughrigg Fell. We returned to supper at ten o'clock. Thomas Ashburner brought us our eighth cart of coals since May 17th.

Sunday 31 August

Anthony Harrison and John left us at half past seven—a very fine morning. A great deal of corn is cut in the vale, and the whole prospect though not tinged with a general autumnal yellow, yet softened down into a mellowness of colouring which seems to impart softness to the forms of hills and mountains. At eleven o'clock Coleridge came when I was walking in the still clear moonshine in the garden. He came over Helvellyn. Wm was gone to bed and John also, worn out with his ride round Coniston. We sat and chatted till half past three, W. in his dressing gown. Coleridge read us a part of 'Christabel'. Talked much about the mountains, etc. etc. Miss Thrale's hatred—Losh's opinion of Southey—the first of poets.

Harvesting in a valley near Lowther, by Peter de Wint

Monday 1 September

We walked in the wood by the lake. W. read 'Joanna' and 'The Fir Grove' to Coleridge. They bathed. The morning was delightful with somewhat of an autumnal freshness. After dinner Coleridge discovered a rock-seat in the orchard. Cleared away the brambles. Coleridge obliged to go to bed after tea. John and I followed Wm up the hill and then returned to go to Mr Simpson's. We borrowed some bottles for bottling rum. The evening somewhat frosty and grey but very pleasant. I broiled Coleridge a mutton chop which he ate in bed. Wm was gone to bed. I chatted with John and Coleridge till near twelve.

Tuesday 2 September

In the morning they all went to Stickel Tarn. A very fine, warm sunny beautiful morning. I baked a pie etc. for dinner—little Sally was with me. The fair-day. Miss Simpson and Mr came down to tea—we walked to the fair. There seemed very few people and very few stalls yet I believe there were many cakes and much beer sold. My brothers came home to dinner at six o'clock. We drank tea immediately after by candlelight. It was a lovely moonlight night. We talked much about a house on Helvellyn. The moonlight shone only upon the village it did not eclipse the village lights and the sound of dancing and merriment came along the still air. I walked with Coleridge and Wm up the lane and by the church, and then lingered with Coleridge in the garden. John and Wm were both gone to bed, and all the lights out.

Wednesday 3 September

Coleridge Wm and John went from home to go upon Helvellyn with Mr Simpson. They set out after breakfast. I accompanied them up near the blacksmith's. A fine coolish morning. I ironed till half past three—now very hot. I then went to a funeral at John Dawson's. About ten men and four women. Bread cheese and ale. They talked sensibly and cheerfully about common things. The dead person 56 years of age buried by the parish. The coffin was neatly lettered and painted black and covered with a decent cloth. They set the corpse down at the door and while we stood within the threshold the men with their hats off sang with decent and solemn countenances a verse of a funeral psalm. The corpse was then borne down the hill and they sang till they had got past the town-end. I was affected to tears while we stood in the house, the coffin lying before me. There were no near kindred, no children. When we got out of the dark house the sun was shining and the prospect looked so divinely beautiful as I never saw it. It seemed more sacred than I had ever seen it, and yet more allied to human life. The green fields, neighbours of the churchyard, were as green as possible and with the brightness of the sunshine looked quite gay. I thought she was going to a quiet spot and I could not help weeping very much. When we came to the bridge they began to sing again and stopped during four lines before they entered the churchyard. The priest met us—he did not look as a man ought to do on such an occasion—I had seen him half-drunk the day before in a pot-house. Before we came with the corpse one of the company observed he wondered what sort of cue 'our parson would be in'. N.B. it was the day after the fair. I had not finished ironing till seven o'clock. The wind was now high and I did not walk—writing my journal now at eight o'clock. Wm and John came home at ten o'clock.

Thursday 4 September

A fine warm day. I was busy all the morning making a mattress. Mr Simpson called in the afternoon. Wm walked in the wood in the morning, and in the evening as we set forward to walk a letter from Mrs Clarkson. We walked into the Black Quarter. The patches of corn very interesting.

Friday 5 September

Finished the mattress, ironed the white bed in the afternoon. When I was putting it up Mr and Mrs Losh arrived while Wm and John were walking.

Saturday 6 September

Breakfasted with the Loshes—very warm—returned through Rydale woods. The Clarksons dined. After tea we walked round Rydale—a little rain.

Sunday 7 September

Rainy. Walked before dinner over the stepping stones to Langdale and home on the other side of the lake. I lay down after dinner. Wm poorly. Walked into the Black Quarter.

Monday 8 September

Very rainy. The Clarksons left us after dinner—still rainy. We walked towards Rydale, and then to Mr Olliff's gate. A fine evening.

Tuesday 9 September

Mr Marshall came—he dined with us. My brothers walked with him round the lakes after dinner—windy—we went to the island. W. and I after to tea. John and I went to the B. Quarter, before supper went to seek a horse at Dawson's—fir grove. After supper, talked of Wm's poems.

Wednesday 10 September

After breakfast Mr Marshall, Wm and John went on horseback to Keswick—I wrote to Mrs Marshall—a fine autumn day. I had a fire. Paid Mr Bousfield eight pounds two and elevenpence. After tea walked with french beans to Mr Simpson's—went up to the forest side above a deserted house, sat till twilight came on. Mr and Miss S. came down with me and supped.

Thursday 11 September

All the morning mending white gown—washed my head—Molly washing. Drank tea at Mr Simpson's. Found Wm at home at my return—he was unable to go on with Mr Marshall and parted from him in Borrowdale. Made tea after my return.

Friday 12 September

I worked in the morning cut my thumb. Walked in the fir grove before dinner—after dinner sat under the trees in the orchard. A rainy morning but very fine afternoon. Miss Simpson called for my packing needle. The fern of the mountains now spreads yellow veins among the trees. The coppice wood turns brown. William observed some affecting little things in Borrowdale. A decayed house with this inscription [*blank space*] in the churchyard, the tall silent rocks seen through the broken windows. A kind of rough column put upon the gavel end of a house with a ball stone smooth from the river placed upon it for ornament. Near it one stone like it upon an old mansion carefully hewn.

Saturday 13 September

William writing his preface did not walk. Jones and Mr Palmer came to tea. We walked with them to Borricks—a lovely evening but the air frosty—worked when I returned home. Wm walked out. John came. Horse from Mr Marshall sent backward to Mrs Clarkson.

Sunday 14 September

Made bread. A sore thumb from a cut. A lovely day—read Boswell in the house in the morning and after dinner under the bright yellow leaves of the orchard. The pear trees a bright yellow, the apple trees green still. A sweet lovely afternoon.

Fern, by William Green

Ullswater, by John White Abbott

Here I have long neglected my journal. John came home in the evening after Jones left us. Jones returned again on the Friday, the 19th September. Jones stayed with us till Friday, 26th September. Coleridge came on Tuesday 23rd and went home with Jones. Charles Lloyd called on Tuesday 23rd, and on Sunday 28th we drank tea and supped with him, and on that day heard of the *Abergavenny*'s arrival. While Jones was with us we had much rainy weather. On Sunday the 21st Tom Myers and father called, and on the 28th Mr and Miss Smith.

On Monday 29th John left us. Wm and I parted with him in sight of Ullswater. It was a fine day, showery but with sunshine and fine clouds. Poor fellow, my heart was right sad—I could not help thinking we should see him again because he was only going to Penrith.

On Tuesday 30th September Charles Lloyd dined with us. We walked homewards with him after dinner. It rained very hard. Rydale was extremely wild and we had a fine walk. We sat quietly and comfortably by the fire. I wrote—the last sheet of Notes and Preface. Went to bed at twelve o'clock.

Wednesday 1 October

A fine morning—a showery night. The lake still in the morning—in the forenoon flashing light from the beams of the sun, as it was ruffled by the wind. We corrected the last sheet.

Thursday 2 October

A very rainy morning. We walked after dinner to observe the torrents. I followed Wm to Rydale, he afterwards went to Butterlip How. I came home to receive the Lloyds. They walked with us to see Churnmilk Force and the Black Quarter. The Black Quarter looked marshy, and the general prospect was cold, but the Force was very grand. The lichens are now coming out afresh, I carried home a collection in the afternoon. We had a pleasant conversation about the manners of the rich—avarice, inordinate desires, and the effeminacy unnaturalness and the unworthy objects of education. After the Lloyds were gone we walked—a showery evening. The moonlight lay upon the hills like snow.

Friday 3 October

Very rainy all the morning. Little Sally learning to mark. Wm walked to Ambleside after dinner. I went with him part of the way—he talked much about the object of his Essay for the second volume of *Lyrical Ballads*. I returned expecting the Simpsons—they did not come. I should have met Wm but my teeth ached and it was showery and late—he returned after ten. Amos Cottle's death in the *Morning Post*. Wrote to S. Lowthian.

N.B. When Wm and I returned from accompanying Jones we met an old man almost double, he had on a coat thrown over his shoulders above his waistcoat and coat. Under this he carried a bundle and had an apron on and a nightcap. His face was interesting. He had dark eyes and a long nose. John who afterwards met him at Wytheburn took him for a Jew. He was of Scotch parents but had been born in the army. He had had a wife 'and a good woman and it pleased God to bless us with ten children'. All these were dead but one of whom he had not heard for many years, a sailor. His trade was to gather leeches, but now leeches are scarce and he had not strength for it. He lived by begging and was making his way to Carlisle where he should buy a few godly books to sell. He said leeches were very scarce partly owing to this dry season, but many years they have been scarce—he supposed it owing to their being much sought after, that they did not breed fast, and were of slow growth. Leeches were formerly two and sixpence a hundred; they are now thirty shillings. He had been hurt in driving a cart, his leg broke his body driven over his skull fractured. He felt no pain till he recovered from his first insensibility. It was then late in the evening, when the light was just going away.

Saturday 4 October

A very rainy, or rather showery and gusty morning for often the sun shines. Thomas Ashburner could not go to Keswick. Read a part of Lamb's play. The language is often very beautiful, but too imitative in particular phrases, words etc. The characters except Margaret's unintelligible, and except Margaret's do not show themselves in action. Coleridge came in while we were at dinner very wet.—We talked till twelve o'clock. He had sat up all the night before writing Essays for the newspaper.—His youngest child had been very ill in convulsion fits. Exceedingly delighted with the second part of 'Christabel'.

Sunday 5 October

Coleridge read a second time 'Christabel'—we had increasing pleasure. A delicious morning. Wm and I were employed all the morning in writing an addition to the Preface. Wm went to bed very ill after working after dinner. Coleridge and I walked to Ambleside after dark with the letter. Returned to tea at nine o'clock. Wm still in bed and very ill. Silver How in both lakes.

Journal entry for 3 October 1800, source of the poem
'Resolution and Independence' ('The Leech Gatherer')

Monday 6 October

A rainy day. Coleridge intending to go but did not get off. We walked after dinner to Rydale. After tea read 'The Pedlar'. Determined not to print 'Christabel' with the *Lyrical Ballads*.

Tuesday 7 October

Coleridge went off at eleven o'clock.—I went as far as Mr Simpson's returned with Mary. She drank tea here. I was very ill in the evening at the Simpsons'—went to bed— supped there. Returned with Miss S. and Mrs J.—heavy showers. Found Wm at home. I was still weak and unwell—went to bed immediately.

Wednesday 8 October

A threatening bad morning—We dried the linen frequent threatening of showers. Received a five pound note from Montagu. Wm walked to Rydale. I copied a part of 'The Beggar' in the morning—I was not quite well in the evening therefore I did not walk— Wm walked. A very mild moonlight night. Glowworms everywhere.

Itinerant, by John Harden

Thursday 9 October

I was ironing all the day till tea time. Very rainy. Wm and I walked in the evening—intending to go to Lloyd's but it came on so very rainy that we were obliged to shelter at Fleming's. A grand ball at Rydale. After sitting some time we went homewards and were again caught by a shower and sheltered under the sycamore at the boat house—a very cold snowlike rain. A man called in a soldier's dress—he was thirty years old, of Cockermouth, had lost a leg and thigh in battle was going to his home. He could earn more money in travelling with his ass than at home.

Friday 10 October

In the morning when I arose the mists were hanging over the opposite hills and the tops of the highest hills were covered with snow. There was a most lovely combination at the head of the vale—of the yellow autumnal hills wrapped in sunshine, and overhung with partial mists, the green and yellow trees and the distant snow-topped mountains. It was a most heavenly morning. The Cockermouth traveller came with thread hardware mustard, etc. She is very healthy; has travelled over the mountains these thirty years. She does not mind the storms if she can keep her goods dry. Her husband will not travel with an ass, because it is the tramper's badge—she would have one to relieve her from the weary load. She was going to Ulverston and was to return to Ambleside Fair. After I had finished baking I went out with Wm Mrs Jameson and Miss Simpson towards Rydale—the fern among the rocks exquisitely beautiful. We turned home and walked to Mr Gell's. After dinner Wm went to bed—I read Southey's letters. Miss Simpson and Mrs Jameson came to tea. After tea we went to Lloyd's—a fine evening as we went but rained in returning—we were wet—found them not at home. I wrote to Mrs Clarkson—sent off 'The Beggar' etc. by Thomas Ashburner who went to fetch our ninth cart of coals. William sat up after me writing 'Point Rash Judgment'.

Saturday 11 October

A fine October morning. Sat in the house working all the morning. Wm composing—Sally Ashburner learning to mark. After dinner we walked up Greenhead Gill in search of a sheepfold. We went by Mr Olliff's and through his woods. It was a delightful day and the views looked excessively cheerful and beautiful chiefly that from Mr Olliff's field where our house is to be built. The colours of the mountains soft and rich, with orange fern—the cattle pasturing upon the hill-tops kites sailing in the sky above our heads—sheep bleating and in lines and chains and patterns scattered over the mountains. They come down and feed on the little green islands in the beds of the torrents and so may be swept away. The sheep-fold is falling away it is built nearly in the form of a heart unequally divided. Look down the brook and see the drops rise upwards and sparkle in the air, at the little falls the higher sparkles the tallest. We walked along the turf of the mountain till we came to a cattle track—made by the cattle which come upon the hills. We drank tea at Mr Simpson's returned at about nine—a fine mild night.

Sunday 12 October

Beautiful day. Sat in the house writing in the morning while Wm went into the wood to compose. Wrote to John in the morning—copied poems for the *Lyrical Ballads*, in the evening wrote to Mrs Rawson. Mary Jameson and Sally Ashburner dined. We pulled apples after dinner, a large basket full. We walked before tea by Bainriggs to observe the many coloured foliage the oaks dark green with yellow leaves, the birches generally still green, some near the water yellowish. The sycamore crimson and crimson-tufted, the mountain ash a deep orange, the common ash lemon colour but many ashes still fresh in their summer green. Those that were discoloured chiefly near the water. William composing in the evening. Went to bed at twelve o'clock.

Monday 13 October

A grey day. Mists on the hills. We did not walk in the morning. I copied poems on the naming of places. A fair at Ambleside. Walked in the Black Quarter at night.

Tuesday 14 October

Wm lay down after dinner—I read Southey's *Spain*. The wind rose very high in the evening. Wm walked out just at bedtime—I went to bed early. We walked before dinner to Rydale.

Wednesday 15 October

A very fine clear morning. After Wm had composed a little, I persuaded him to go into the orchard. We walked backwards and forwards. The prospect most divinely beautiful from the seat—all colours, all melting into each other. I went in to put bread in the oven and we both walked within view of Rydale. Wm again composed at 'The Sheep-fold' after dinner. I walked with him to Wytheburn, and he went on to Keswick. I drank tea and supped at Mr Simpson's—a very cold frosty air, and a spangled sky in returning. Mr and Miss S. came with me. Wytheburn looked very wintry but yet there was a foxglove blossoming by the roadside.

Thursday 16 October

A very fine morning—starched and hung out linen a very fine day. John Fisher, T. A., S. A. and Molly working in the garden. Wrote to Miss Nicholson. I walked as far as Rydale between three and four—ironed till six—got tea and wrote to Mr Griffith. A letter from Mr Clarkson.

Friday 17 October

A very fine grey morning. The swan hunt. Sally working in the garden. I walked round the lake between a quarter past twelve and half past one. Wrote to M. H. After dinner I walked to Lloyd's—carried my letters to Miss N. and M. H. The Lloyds not in—I waited for them. Charles not well. Letters from M. H., Biggs and John. In my walk in the

Borrowdale, by John Constable

morning, I observed Benson's honeysuckles in flower, and great beauty. It was a very fine mild evening. Ll.'s servants came with me to Parke's. I found Wm at home where he had been almost ever since my departure. Coleridge had done nothing for the *Lyrical Ballads*. Working hard for Stuart. Glowworms in abundance.

Saturday 18 October

A very fine October morning. William worked all the morning at 'The Sheep-fold' but in vain. He lay down in the afternoon till seven o'clock but could not sleep—I slept. My head better—he unable to work. We did not walk all day.

Sunday 19 October

We rose late and walked directly after breakfast. The tops of Grasmere mountains cut off. Rydale was very very beautiful the surface of the water quite still like a dim mirror. The colours of the large island exquisitely beautiful and the trees still fresh and green were magnified by the mists. The prospects on the west side of the lake were very beautiful. We sat at the two points looking up to Park's. The lowing of the cattle was echoed by a hollow voice in Nab Scar. We went upon Loughrigg Fell—and were disappointed with Grasmere, it did not look near so beautiful as Rydale. We returned home over the stepping stones. Wm got to work. We are not to dine till four o'clock.— Dined at half past five—Mr Simpson dined and drank tea with us. We went to bed immediately after he left us.

Monday 20 October

William worked in the morning at 'The Sheep-fold'. After dinner we walked to Rydale crossed the stepping stones and while we were walking under the tall oak trees the Lloyds called out to us. They went with us on the western side of Rydale. The lights were very grand upon the woody Rydale Hills. Those behind dark and topped with clouds. The two lakes were divinely beautiful. Grasmere excessively solemn and the whole lake was calm and dappled with soft grey ripples. The Lloyds stayed with us till eight o'clock. We then walked to the top of the hill at Rydale. Very mild and warm. About six glowworms shining faintly. We went up as far as the grove. When we came home the fire was out. We ate our supper in the dark and went to bed immediately. William was disturbed in the night by the rain coming into his room, for it was a very rainy night. The ash leaves lay across the road.

Tuesday 21 October

We walked in the morning past Mr Gell's—a very fine clear sharp sunny morning. We drank tea at the Lloyds. It was very cold in the evening, quite frosty, and starlight. Wm had been unsuccessful in the morning at 'The Sheep-fold'. The reflection of the ash scattered, and the tree stripped.

Wednesday 22 October

We walked to Mr Gell's a very fine morning. Wm composed without much success at 'The Sheep-Fold'. Coleridge came in to dinner. He had done nothing. We were very merry. C. and I went to look at the prospect from his seat. In the evening Stoddart came in when we were at tea, and after tea Mr and Miss Simpson with large potatoes and plums. Wm read after supper, 'Ruth' etc.—Coleridge 'Christabel'.

Mr Gell's cottage, by John Harden

Thursday 23 October

Coleridge and Stoddart went to Keswick. We accompanied them to Wytheburn. A wintry grey morning—from the top of the Rays Grasmere looked like winter and Wytheburn still more so. We called upon Mrs Simpson and sat ten minutes in returning. Wm was not successful in composition in the evening.

Oak tree in Rydale Park, by William Green

Friday 24 October

A very fine morning. We walked before Wm began to work to the top of the Rydale Hill. He was afterwards only partly successful in composition. After dinner we walked round Rydale Lake, rich, calm, streaked, very beautiful. We went to the top of Loughrigg. Grasmere sadly inferior. We were much tired Wm went to bed till half past seven. The ash in our garden green, one close to it bare, the next nearly so.

Saturday 25 October

A very rainy day. Wm again unsuccessful. We could not walk it was so very rainy. We read Rogers, Miss Seward, Cowper etc.

Sunday 26 October

Heavy rain all night. A fine morning after ten o'clock. Wm composed a good deal—in the morning. The Lloyds came to dinner and were caught in a shower. Wm read some of his poems after dinner. A terrible night. I went with Mrs Lloyd to Newton's to see for lodgings. Mr Simpson in coming from Ambleside called in for a glass of rum, just before we went to bed.

Monday 27 October

A rainy morning. The hilltops covered with snow. Charles Lloyd came for his wife's glass. I walked home with him past Rydale. When he came I met him as I was carrying some cold meat to Wm in the fir grove. I had before walked with him there for some time. It was a fine shelter from the wind. The coppices now nearly of one brown. An oak tree in a sheltered place near John Fisher's—not having lost any of its leaves was quite brown and dry. We did not walk after dinner. It was a fine wild moonlight night. Wm could not compose much fatigued himself with altering.

Tuesday 28 October

A very rainy night. I was baking bread in the morning and made a giblet pie. We walked out before dinner to our favourite field. The mists sailed along the mountains and rested upon them enclosing the whole vale. In the evening the Lloyds came. We drank tea with them at Borrick's and played a rubber at whist—stayed supper. Wm looked very well. A fine moonlight night when we came home.

Card players, by John Harden

Wednesday 29 October

William working at his poem all the morning. After dinner Mr Clarkson called. We went down to Borrick's and he and the Lloyds and Priscilla came back to drink tea with us. We met Stoddart upon the bridge. Played at cards. The Lloyds etc. went home to supper—Mr Clarkson slept here.

Sketch at Borrowdale, by John Constable

Thursday 30 October

A rainy morning. Mr C. went over Kirkstone. Wm talked all day and almost all night with Stoddart. Mrs and Miss Ll. called in the morning. I walked with them to Tail End. A fine pleasant morning but a very rainy afternoon. W. and S. in the house all day.

Friday 31 October

W. and S. did not rise till one o'clock. W. very sick and very ill. S. and I drank tea at Lloyd's and came home immediately after. A very fine moonlight night—the moonshine like herrings in the water.

Saturday 1 November

William better. We met as we walked to Rydale a boy from Lloyd's, coming for *Don Quixote*. Talk in the evening. Tom Ashburner brought our tenth cart of coals.

Sunday 2 November

We walked into the Black Quarter. A very fine morning. A succession of beautiful views mists etc. etc. Much rain in the night. In the evening drank tea at Lloyd's—found them all ill in colds. Came home to supper.

Monday 3 November

Walked to Rydale. A cold day. Wm and Stoddart still talking, frequent showers in our walk. In the evening we talked merrily over the fire. The Speddings stopped at the door.

Tuesday 4 November

Stoddart left us—I walked a little way with W. and him, W. went to the tarn afterwards to the top of Seat Sandal. He was obliged to lie down in the tremendous wind. The snow blew from Helvellyn horizontally like smoke—the spray of the unseen waterfall like smoke.—Miss Lloyd called upon me—I walked with her past Rydale. Wm sadly tired, threatening of the piles.

Rothay Bridge, by John Harden

Wednesday 5 November

Wm not well. A very fine beautiful clear winter's day. I walked after dinner to Lloyd's—drank tea and Mrs and Miss Lloyd came to Rydale with me. The moon was rising but the sky all over cloud. I made tea for William. Piles.

Thursday 6 November

A very rainy morning and night. I was baking bread dinner and parkins. Charles and P. Lloyd called. Wm somewhat better read 'Point Rash Judgment'. The lake calm and very beautiful. A very rainy afternoon and night.

Friday 7 November

A cold rainy morning. Wm still unwell. I working and reading *Amelia*. The Michaelmas daisy droops, the pansies are full of flowers. The ashes opposite are green all but one but they have lost many of their leaves. The copses are quite brown. The poor woman and child from Whitehaven drank tea—nothing warm that day. A very rainy morning. It cleared up in the afternoon. We expected the Lloyds but they did not come. Wm still unwell. A rainy night.

Saturday 8 November

A rainy morning. A whirlwind came that tossed about the leaves and tore off the still green leaves of the ashes. A fine afternoon. Wm and I walked out at four o'clock. Went as far as Rothay Bridge. Met the butcher's man with a letter from 'Monk' Lewis. The country very wintry—some oaks quite bare—others more sheltered with a few green leaves others with brown leaves, but the whole face of the country in a winter covering. We went early to bed.

Sunday 9 November

Wm slept tolerably—better this morning. It was a frosty night. We walked to Rydale after dinner, partly expecting to meet the Lloyds. Mr Simpson brought newspapers but met Molly with them. W. burnt 'The Sheep-fold'. A rainy night.

Monday 10 November

I baked bread. A fine clear frosty morning. We walked after dinner—to Rydale village. Jupiter over the hilltops, the only star like a sun flashed out at intervals from behind a black cloud.

Tuesday 11 November

Walked to Rydale before dinner for letters. William had been working at 'The Sheep-fold'. They were salving sheep. A rainy morning. The Lloyds drank tea with us. Played at cards—Priscilla not well. We walked after they left us to the top of the Rydale Hill then towards Mr Olliff's and towards the village. A mild night partly cloudy partly starlight. The cottage lights, the mountains not very distinct.

Wednesday 12 November

We sat in the house all the day. Mr Simpson called and found us at dinner—a rainy evening—he stayed the evening and supper. I lay down after dinner with a headache.

Thursday 13 November

A stormy night. We sat in the house all the morning. Rainy weather. Old Mr Simpson, Mrs J. and Miss S. drank tea and supped, played at cards, found us at dinner. A poor woman from Hawkshead begged, a widow of Grasmere a merry African from Longtown.

Friday 14 November

I had a bad headache. Much wind but a sweet mild morning. I nailed up trees. Sent Molly Ashburner to excuse us to Lloyd's. Two letters from Coleridge—very ill. One from Sara H., one from S. Lowthian—I wrote to S. Hutchinson and received three pounds from her.

Saturday 15 November

A terrible rain so Wm prevented from going to Coleridge's. The afternoon fine and mild I walked to the top of the hill for a headache. We both set forward at five o'clock after tea. A fine wild but not cold night. I walked with him over the Rays—it was starlight. I parted with him very sad unwilling not to go on. The hills and the stars and the white waters with their ever varying yet ceaseless sound were very impressive. I supped at the Simpsons'. Mr S. walked home with me.

Sunday 16 November

A very fine warm sunny morning. A letter from Coleridge and one from Stoddart. Coleridge better— —My head aching very much I sent to excuse myself to Lloyd's—then walked to the cottage beyond Mr Gell's. One beautiful ash tree sheltered with yellow leaves—one low one quite green. Some low ashes green—a noise of boys in the rocks hunting some animal. Walked a little in the garden when I came home, very pleasant. Now rain came on. Mr Jackson called in the evening when I was at tea brought me a letter from C. and W. C. better.

Monday 17 November

A fine clear frosty morning with a sharp wind. I walked to Keswick. Set off at five minutes past ten, and arrived at half past two. I found them all well.

On Tuesday morning W. and C. set off towards Penrith. Wm met Sara Hutchinson at Threlkeld. They arrived at Keswick at tea time.

Wednesday 19 November

We walked by the lakeside and they went to Mr Denton's. I called upon the Miss Cockins.

Thursday 20 November

We spent the morning in the town. Mr Jackson and Mr Peach dined with us.

Friday 21 November

A very fine day. Went to Mrs Greaves. Mrs C. and I called upon the Speddings. A beautiful crescent moon.

Saturday 22 November

After visiting Mr Peach's Chinese pictures we set off to Grasmere. A threatening and rather rainy morning. Arrived at G. very dirty and a little wet at the closing in of evening. Wm not quite well.

Sunday 23 November

Wm not well. I baked bread and pie for dinner. Sara and I walked after dinner and met Mr Gawthorpe, paid his bill and he drank tea with us paid five pounds for Mr Bousfield.

Monday 24 November

A fine morning, Sara and I walked to Rydale. After dinner we went to Lloyd's and drank tea, and supped. A sharp cold night with sleet and snow. I had the toothache in the night. Took laudanum.

Tuesday 25 November

Very ill—in bed all day—better in the evening. I read *Tom Jones*—very sleepy slept all night.

Wednesday 26 November

Well in the morning. Wm very well. We had a delightful walk up into Easedale. The tops of the mountains covered with snow—frosty and sunny—the roads slippy. A letter from Mary. The Lloyds drank tea. We walked with them near to Ambleside. A beautiful moonlight night. Sara and I walked before dinner. William very well and highly poetical.

William Wordsworth in 1805, by Henry Edridge

Skiddaw and Derwentwater, by Thomas Sunderland

Thursday 27 November

Wrote to Tom Hutchinson to desire him to bring Mary with him from Stockton. A thaw and the ground covered with snow. Sara and I walked before dinner.

Friday 28 November

Coleridge walked over. Miss Simpson drank tea with us. William walked home with her. Coleridge was very unwell. He went to bed before Wm's return. Great boils upon his neck.

Saturday 29 November

A fine day.

Sunday 30 November

A very fine clear morning. Snow upon the ground everywhere. Sara and I walked towards Rydale by the upper road and were obliged to return because of the snow; walked by moonlight.

Monday 1 December

A thaw in the night and the snow was entirely gone. Sara and I had a delightful walk by the upper Rydale road and Mr King's. Coleridge unable to go home for his health. We walked by moonlight. Baking day little loaves.

Tuesday 2 December

A rainy morning. Coleridge was obliged to set off. Sara and I met C. Lloyd and P.—turned back with them. I walked round the two lakes with Charles very pleasant—passing lights—I was sadly wet when we came home and very cold. Priscilla drank tea with us. We all walked to Ambleside. A pleasant moonlight evening but not clear. Supped upon a hare. It came on a terrible evening hail and wind and cold and rain.

Wednesday 3 December

We lay in bed till eleven o'clock. Wrote to John, and M. H. William and Sara and I walked to Rydale after tea—a very fine frosty night. Sara and W. walked round the other side. I was tired and returned home. We went to bed early.

Thursday 4 December

Coleridge came in just as we finished dinner—pork from the Simpsons. Sara and I walked round the two lakes—a very fine morning. C. ate nothing to cure his boils. We walked after tea by moonlight to look at Langdale covered with snow—the Pikes not grand, but the Old Man very impressive. Cold and slippery but exceedingly pleasant. Sat up till half past one.

Friday 5 December

Terribly cold and rainy. Coleridge and Wm set forward towards Keswick but the wind in Coleridge's eyes made him turn back. Sara and I had a grand bread and cake baking. We were very merry in the evening but grew sleepy soon though we did not go to bed till twelve o'clock.

Saturday 6 December

Wm accompanied Coleridge to the foot of the Rays. A very pleasant morning. Sara and I accompanied him halfway to Keswick. Thirlmere was very beautiful—even more so than in summer. William was not well had laboured unsuccessfully. Charles Lloyd had called. Sara and I drank tea with Mrs Simpson. A sharp shower met us—it rained a little when we came home. Mr B. S. accompanied us. Miss S. at Ambleside. William tired and not well. A letter from M. H.

Leathes Water, Thirlmere, by John Constable

Greta Hall and Keswick Bridge, by William Westall

Sunday 7 December

A fine morning. I read. Sara wrote to Hartley, Wm to Mary, I to Mrs C. We walked just before dinner to the lakeside and found out a seat in a tree windy but pleasant. Sara and Wm walked to the waterfalls at Rydale. I was unwell and went to bed till eight o'clock—a pleasant mild evening. Went to bed at twelve. Miss Simpson called.

Monday 8 December

A sweet mild morning.—I wrote to Mrs Cookson and Miss Griffith.

Tuesday 9 December

I dined at Lloyd's. Wm drank tea. Walked home. A pleasant starlight frosty evening. Reached home at one o'clock. Wm finished his poem today.

Wednesday 10 December

Walked to Keswick. Snow upon the ground. A very fine day. Ate bread and ale at John Stanley's. Found Coleridge better. Stayed at Keswick till Sunday 14th December.

Monday 15 December

Baking and starching.

Tuesday 16 December

Ironing—the Lloyds called.

Wednesday 17 December

A very fine day. Writing all the morning for William.

Thursday 18 December

Mrs Coleridge and Derwent came. Sweeping chimneys.

Friday 19 December

Baking.

Saturday 20 December

Coleridge came. Very ill rheumatic, feverish. Rain incessantly.

Monday 22 December

S. and Wm went to Lloyd's. Wm dined, it rained very hard when he came home.

Scullery maid, by John Harden

· *1801* ·

Saturday 10 October

Coleridge went to Keswick after we had built Sara's seat.

Sunday 11 October

Mr and Miss Simpson came in after tea and supped with us.

Monday 12 October

We drank tea at Mr Simpson's.

Tuesday 13 October

A thorough wet day.

Thursday 15 October

We dined at Mr Luff's. A rainy morning. Coleridge came into Mr L.'s while we were at dinner. Wm and I walked up Loughrigg Fell then by the waterside. I held my head under a spout. Very sick and ill when I got home—went to bed in the sitting room—took laudanum.

Friday 16 October

Tom Hutchinson came. It rained almost all day. Coleridge poorly.

Saturday 17 October

We walked into Easedale. Coleridge poorly after dinner.

Waterfall near Sourmilk Gill, Easedale, by Rev. Thomas Austin

Sunday 18 October

I have forgotten.

Monday 19 October

Coleridge went home. Tom and William walked to Rydale—a very fine day. I was ill in bed all day. Mr Simpson tea and supper.

Tuesday 20 October

We went to the Langdales and Colleth—a very fine day; a heavy shower in the afternoon in Langdale.

Wednesday 21 October

Dined at Bowness, slept at Penny Bridge—in danger of being cast away on Windermere. A very fine day, but windy a little—a moonlight night.

Thursday 22 October

Breakfasted at Penny Bridge—dined at Coniston—a grand stormy day—drank tea at home.

Friday 23 October

A sweet delightful morning. I planted all sorts of plants, Tom helped me. He and W. then rode to Hawkshead. I baked bread and pies. Tom brought me two shrubs from Mr Curwen's nursery.

Saturday 24 October

Attempted Fairfield but misty and we went no further than Green Head Gill to the sheep-fold. Mild misty beautiful soft. Wm and Tom put out the boat—brought the coat from Mr Luff's. Mr Simpson came in at dinner time—drank tea with us and played at cards.

Sunday 25 October

Rode to Legberthwaite with Tom—expecting Mary—sweet day. Went upon Helvellyn, glorious glorious sights. The sea at Cartmel. The Scotch mountains beyond the sea to the right. Whiteside large and round and very soft and green behind us. Mists above and below and close to us, with the sun amongst them—they shot down to the coves. Left John Stanley's at ten minutes past twelve. Returned thither quarter past four—drank tea ate heartily. Before we went on Helvellyn we got bread and cheese—paid four shillings for the whole—reached home at nine o'clock. A soft grey evening—the light of the moon but she did not shine on us.

Helvellyn, by John Constable

Buttermere Bridge, by John Glover

Monday 26 October

Omitted. They went to Buttermere.

Tuesday 27 October

Omitted, drank tea at Mr Simpson's.

Wednesday 28 October

The Clarksons came.

Thursday 29 October

Rain all day.

Friday 30 October

Rain all day.

Saturday 31 October

We walked to Rydale—a soft and mild morning but threatening for rain.

Sunday 1 November

Very cold—we walked in the evening to Butterlip How.

Monday 2 November

Very rainy.

Tuesday 3 November

We dined at Lloyd's. Cold and clear day.

Wednesday 4 November

Mr C. and Wm rode out—very cold.

Monday 9 November

Walked with Coleridge to Keswick . . . the mountains for ever varying, now hid in the clouds and now with their tops visible while perhaps they were half concealed below—Legberthwaite beautiful. We ate bread and cheese at John Stanley's and reached Keswick without fatigue just before dark. We enjoyed ourselves in the study and were *at home*. Supped at Mr Jackson's. Mary and I sat in C.'s room a while.

Tuesday 10 November

Poor C. left us and we came home together. We left Keswick at two o'clock and did not arrive at G. till nine o'clock. Drank tea at John Stanley's very comfortably. I burnt myself with Coleridge's aquafortis. Mary's feet sore. C. had a sweet day for his ride. Every sight and every sound reminded me of him dear dear fellow—of his many walks to us by day and by night—of all dear things. I was melancholy and could not talk, but at last I eased my heart by weeping—nervous blubbering says William. It is not so. O how many, many reasons have I to be anxious for him.

aquafortis: nitric acid

Samuel Taylor Coleridge in 1804, by George Dance

Wednesday 11 November

Baked bread and giblet pie—put books in order—mended stockings. Put aside dearest C.'s letters, and now at about seven o'clock we are all sitting by a nice fire—W. with his book and a candle and Mary writing to Sara.

Thursday 12 November

A beautiful still sunshiny morning. We rose very late. I put the rag boxes into order. We walked out while the goose was roasting—we walked to the top of the hill. M. and I followed Wm—he was walking upon the turf between John's Grove and the lane. It was a most sweet noon. We did not go into John's Grove, but we walked among the rocks and there we sat. Mr Olliff passed Mary and me upon the road—Wm still among the rocks. The lake beautiful from the orchard. Wm and I walked out before tea—the crescent moon—we sat in the slate quarry—I sat there a long time alone. Wm reached home before me—I found them at tea. There were a thousand stars in the sky.

Friday 13 November

Dullish, damp and cloudy—a day that promises not to dry our clothes—we spent a happy evening—went to bed late, and had a restless night—Wm better than I expected.

Saturday 14 November

Still a cloudy dull day, very dark. I lay in bed all the day very unwell: they made me some broth and I rose better after it was dark. We spent a quiet evening by the fire.

Sunday 15 November

I walked in the morning to Churnmilk Force nearly, and went upon Heifer crags. The

Limekilns and slate wharf, Clappersgate, by John Harden

Sty Head Tarn, by John Constable

valley of its winter yellow, but the bed of the brook still in some places almost *shaded* with leaves—the oaks brown in general but one that might be almost called green—the whole prospect was very soft and the distant view down the vale very impressive, a long vale down to Ambleside—the hills at Ambleside in mist and sunshine—all else grey. We sat by the fire and read Chaucer (Thomson, Mary read) and Bishop Hall. Letters from Sara and Mrs Clarkson late at night.

Monday 16 November

A very dankish misty wettish morning. Mary and Molly ironed all day. I made bread and called at Mr Olliff's—Mrs O. at home—the prospect soft from the windows. Mrs O. observed that it was beautiful *even* in winter! The Luffs passed us. We walked backwards and forwards in the church field. Wm somewhat weakish, but upon the whole pretty well—he is now at seven o'clock reading Spenser. Mary is writing beside me. The little syke murmurs. We are quiet and happy, but poor Peggy Ashburner is very ill and in pain. She coughs as if she would cough her life away. I am going to write to Coleridge and Sara. Poor C.! I hope he was in London yesterday. Molly has been very witty with Mary all day. She says, 'Ye may say what ye will but there's nothing like a gay auld man for behaving weel to a young wife. Ye may laugh but this wind blows no favour—and where there's no love there's no favour.' On Sunday I lectured little John Dawson for telling lies. I told him I had heard that he charged Jenny Baty falsely with having beaten him. Says Molly: 'she says it's not so that she never lifted hand till him, and she *should* speak truth you would think in her condition'—she is with child. Two beggars today.

syke: stream

Tuesday 17 November

A very rainy morning we walked into Easedale before dinner. Miss S. came in at dinner time—we went to Mr Gell's cottage—then returned. The coppices a beautiful brown, the oaks having a very fine leafy shade. We stood a long time to look at the corner birch tree. The wind was among the light thin twigs, and they yielded to it this way and that. Drank tea and supped at the Simpsons'—a moonlight wettish night. Dirty roads.

Grasmere Church and Bridge, by Rev. Thomas Austin

Wednesday 18 November

We sat in the house in the morning reading Spenser. I was unwell and lay in bed all the afternoon. Wm and Mary walked to Rydale. Very pleasant moonlight. The lakes beautiful. The church an image of peace. Wm wrote some lines upon it. I in bed when they came home. Mary and I walked as far as Sara's Gate before supper. We stood there a long time, the whole scene impressive, the mountains indistinct the lake calm and partly ruffled—large island, a sweet sound of water falling into the quiet lake. A storm was gathering in Easedale so we returned but the moon came out and opened to us the church and village. Helm Crag in shade, the larger mountains dappled like a sky. We stood long upon the bridge. Wished for Wm, he had stayed at home being sickish—found him better. We went to bed.

Thursday 19 November

A beautiful sunny, frosty morning. We did not walk all day. Wm said he would put it off till the fine moonlight night and then it came on a heavy rain and wind. Charles and Olivia Lloyd called in the morning.

Friday 20 November

We walked in the morning to Easedale. In the evening we had cheerful letters from Coleridge and Sara.

Saturday 21 November

We walked in the morning and paid one pound and fourpence for letters. William out of spirits. We had a pleasant walk and spent a pleasant evening. There was a furious wind and cold at night. Mr Simpson drank tea with us and helped William out with the boat.

Wm and Mary walked to The Swan homewards with him. A keen clear frosty night. I went into the orchard while they were out.

Sunday 22 November

We wrote to Coleridge—sent our letter by the boy. Mr and Miss Simpson came in at tea time. We went with them to the blacksmith's and returned by Butterlip How—a frost and wind with bright moonshine. The vale looked spacious and very beautiful—the level meadows seemed very large, and some nearer us unequal ground heaving like sand, the cottages beautiful and quiet. We passed one near which stood a cropped ash with upright forked branches like the devil's horns frightening a guilty conscience. We were happy and cheerful when we came home—we went early to bed.

Monday 23 November

A beautiful frosty morning. Mary was making William's woollen waistcoat. Wm unwell and did not walk. Mary and I sat in our cloaks upon the bench in the orchard. After dinner I went to bed unwell. Mary had a headache at night. We all went to bed soon.

Study at Rydale, by William Green

Tuesday 24 November

A rainy morning. We all were well except that my head ached a little and I took my breakfast in bed. I read a little of Chaucer, prepared the goose for dinner, and then we all walked out. I was obliged to return for my fur tippet and spencer it was so cold. We had intended going to Easedale but we shaped our course to Mr Gell's cottage. It was very windy and we heard the wind everywhere about us as we went along the lane but the walls sheltered us. John Green's house looked pretty under Silver How. As we were going along we were stopped at once, at the distance perhaps of fifty yards from our

Study of trees, by John Constable

favourite birch tree. It was yielding to the gusty wind with all its tender twigs, the sun shone upon it and it glanced in the wind like a flying sunshiny shower. It was a tree in shape with stem and branches but it was like a spirit of water. The sun went in and it resumed its purplish appearance the twigs still yielding to the wind but not so visibly to us. The other birch trees that were near it looked bright and cheerful, but it was a creature by its own self among them. We could not get into Mr Gell's grounds—the old tree fallen from its undue exaltation above the gate. A shower came on when we were at Benson's. We went through the wood—it became fair—there was a rainbow which spanned the lake from the island house to the foot of Bainriggs. The village looked populous and beautiful. Catkins are coming out palm trees budding—the alder with its plum-coloured buds. We came home over the stepping stones. The lake was foamy with white waves. I saw a solitary butterflower in the wood. *I* found it not easy to get over the stepping stones. Reached home at dinner time. Sent Peggy Ashburner some goose. She sent me some honey—with a thousand thanks. 'Alas! the gratitude of men has etc.' I went in to set her right about this and sat a while with her. She talked about Thomas's having sold his land. 'Ay,' says she I said many a time, 'He's not come fra London to buy our land however.' Then she told me with what pains and industry they had made up their taxes interest etc. etc.—how they all got up at five o'clock in the morning to spin and Thomas carded, and that they had paid off a hundred pound of the interest. She said she used to take such pleasure in the cattle and sheep. 'O how pleased I used to be when they fetched them down, and when I had been a bit poorly I would gang out upon a hill and look over t' fields and see them and it used to do me so much good you cannot think.' Molly said to me when I came in, 'Poor body. She's very ill but one does not know how long she may last. Many a fair face may gang before her.' We sat by the fire without work for some time then Mary read a poem of Daniell upon learning. After tea Wm read Spenser now and then a little aloud to us. We were making his waistcoat. We had a note from Mrs C., with bad news from poor C. very ill. William walked to John's Grove. I went to meet him—moonlight but it rained. I met him before I had got as far as John Baty's—he had been surprised and terrified by a sudden rushing of winds which seemed to bring earth sky and lake together, as if the whole were going to enclose him in—he was glad he was in a high road.

In speaking of our walk on Sunday evening the 22nd November I forgot to notice one most impressive sight. It was the moon and the moonlight seen through hurrying driving clouds immediately behind the Stone Man upon the top of the hill on the forest side. Every tooth and every edge of rock was visible, and the Man stood like a giant watching from the roof of a lofty castle. The hill seemed perpendicular from the darkness below it. It was a sight that I could call to mind at any time it was so distinct.

Wednesday 25 November

It was a showery morning and threatened to be a wettish day, but the sun shone once or twice. We were engaged to the Lloyds and Wm and Mary were determined to go that it might be over. I accompanied them to the thorn beside Rydale Water. I parted from them first at the top of the hill and they called me back. It rained a little and rained afterwards all the afternoon. I baked pies and bread, and wrote to Sara Hutchinson and Coleridge. I passed a pleasant evening but the wind roared so and it was such a storm that I was afraid for them. They came in at nine o'clock no worse for their walk and cheerful blooming and happy.

Langdale Pikes, as seen above Skelwith Force, by Edward Lear

Thursday 26 November

Mr Olliff called before Wm was up to say that they would drink tea with us this afternoon. We walked into Easedale to gather mosses and to fetch cream. I went for the cream and they sat under a wall. It was piercing cold and a hail storm came on in the afternoon. The Olliffs arrived at five o'clock. We played cards and passed a decent evening. It was a very still night but piercing cold. When they went away at eleven o'clock, a shower came on.

Friday 27 November

Snow upon the ground thinly scattered. It snowed after we got up and then the sun shone and it was very warm though frosty—now the sun shines sweetly. A woman came who was travelling with her husband—he had been wounded and was going with her to live at Whitehaven. She had been at Ambleside the night before, offered fourpence at The Cock for a bed—they sent her to one Harrison's where she and her husband had slept upon the hearth and bought a pennyworth of chips for a fire. Her husband was gone before very lame—'Aye,' says she, 'I was once an officer's wife I, as you see me now. My first husband married me at Appleby. I had eighteen pounds a year for teaching a school and because I had no fortune his father turned him out of doors. I have been in the West Indies. I lost the use of this finger just before he died he came to me and said he must bid farewell to his dear children and me. I had a muslin gown on like yours—I seized hold of his coat as he went from me and slipped the joint of my finger. He was shot directly. I came to London and married this man. He was clerk to Judge Chambray, *that man*, that man that's going on the road now. If he, Judge Chambray, had been at Kendal he would have given us a guinea or two and made nought of it, for he is very generous.' Before dinner we set forward to walk intending to return to dinner. But as we had got as far as

Rydale Wm thought he would go on to Mr Luff's. We accompanied him under Loughrigg, and parted near the stepping stones. It was very cold. Mary and I walked quick home. There was a fine gleam of sunshine upon the eastern side of Ambleside vale. We came up the old road and turning round we were struck with the appearance. Mary wrote to her aunt. We expected the Simpsons. I was sleepy and weary and went to bed—before tea. It came on wet in the evening and was very cold. We expected letters from C. and Sara—Sara's came by the boy. But none from C.—a sad disappointment. We did not go to meet Wm as we had intended—Mary was at work at Wm's warm waistcoat.

Saturday 28 November

A very fine sunny morning. Soldiers still going by. I should have mentioned that yesterday when we went with Wm to Mr Luff's we met a soldier and his wife, he with a child in his arms, she carrying a bundle and his gun—we gave them some halfpence it was such a pretty sight. William having slept ill lay in bed till after one o'clock. Mary and I walked up to Mr Simpson's between twenty minutes before two and twenty minutes before three to desire them not to come. We drank tea and supped at Mr Olliff's—a keen frost with sparkling stars when we came home at half past eleven.

Sunday 29 November

Baking bread apple pies, and giblet pie—a bad giblet pie. It was a most beautiful morning. George Olliff brought Wm's stick. The sun shone all the day, but we never walked. In the evening we had intended going for letters but the lad said he would go. We sat up till after one—no letters! Very cold—hard frost.

Itinerants selling hamsters, by John Harden

Itinerants, by John Harden

Monday 30 November

A fine sharp morning. The lad brought us a letter from Montagu and a short one from Coleridge, C. very well—promised to write tomorrow. We walked round the lake. Wm and Mary went first over the stepping stones. I remained after them and went into the prospect field above Benson's to sit—Mary joined me there. Clear and frosty without wind. William went before to look at Langdale. We saw the Pikes and then came home. They have cropped the tree which over-shadowed the gate beside that cottage at the turning of the hill which used to make a frame for Loughrigg Tarn and Windermere. We came home and read. Mary wrote to Joanna—I wrote to Richard, and Mrs Coleridge.

Tuesday 1 December

A fine sunny and frosty morning. Mary and I walked to Rydale for letters, William was not well and stayed at home reading after having lain long in bed. We found a letter from Coleridge, a short one—he was pretty well. We were overtaken by two soldiers on our return—one of them being very drunk we wished them to pass us, but they had too much liquor in them to go very fast so we contrived to pass them—they were very merry and very civil. They fought with the mountains with their sticks. Aye says one, that will upon us. One might stride over that etc. They never saw such a wild country though one of them was a Scotchman. They were honest looking fellows. The Corporal said he was frightened to see the road before them. We met Wm at Sara's gate. He went back intending to go round the lake but having attempted to cross the water and not succeeding he came back. The Simpsons Mr and Miss drank tea with us—Wm was very poorly and out of spirits. They stayed supper.

Wednesday 2 December

A fine grey frosty morning. Wm rose late. I read the tale of Phœbus and the Crow which he afterwards attempted to translate and did translate a large part of it today. Mrs Olliff brought us some yeast and made us promise to go there the next day to meet the Luffs. We were sitting by the fire in the evening when Charles and Olivia Lloyd came in. I had not been very well so I did not venture out with them when they went away—Mary and William went as far as Rydale village. It snowed after it was dark, and there was a thin covering over the ground which made it light and soft. They looked fresh and well when they came in. I wrote part of a letter to Coleridge. After his return William went on a little with Chaucer.

Thursday 3 December

I was not well in the morning. We baked bread—after dinner I went to bed—William walked into Easedale. Rain, hail and snow. I rose at half past seven, got tea, then went to sup at Mr Olliff's—I had a glorious sleep and was quite well. A light night roads very slippery. We spent a pleasant evening—Mr and Mrs Luff there—Mrs L. poorly. I wrote a little bit of my letter to Coleridge before I went to Mr O.'s. We went to bed immediately after our return—Molly gone.

Friday 4 December

My head bad and I lay long. Mrs Luff called—Mary went with her to the slate quarry. Mr Simpson and Charles Lloyd called for the yeast receipt. William translating 'The Prioress's Tale'. William and Mary walked after tea to Rydale. It snowed and rained and they came in wet. I finished the letter to Coleridge and we received a letter from him and Sara. S.'s letter written in good spirits—C.'s also. A letter of Lamb's about George Dyer with it.

Saturday 5 December

My head bad and I lay long. Mr Luff called before I rose. We put off walking in the morning: dull and misty and grey—very rainy in the afternoon and we could not go out. William finished 'The Prioress's Tale', and after tea Mary and he wrote it out. Wm not well.—No parcel from Mrs Coleridge.

Sunday 6 December

A very fine beautiful sunshiny morning. William worked a while at Chaucer, then we set forward to walk into Easedale. We met Mr and Mrs Olliff who were going to call upon us. They turned back with us and we parted at the White Bridge. We went up in to Easedale and walked backwards and forwards in that flat field which makes the second area of Easedale with that beautiful rock in the field beside us and all the rocks and the woods and the mountains enclosing us round. The sun was shining among them, the snow thinly scattered upon the tops of the mountains. In the afternoon we sat by the fire—I read Chaucer aloud, and Mary read the first canto of 'The Faerie Queene'. After tea Mary and I walked to Ambleside for letters—reached home by eleven o'clock. We had a sweet walk. It was a sober starlight evening, the stars not shining as it were with all their brightness when they were visible and sometimes hiding themselves behind small greyish clouds that passed soberly along. We opened C.'s letter at Wilcock's door we thought we saw that he wrote in good spirits so we came happily homewards where we arrived two hours after we left home. It was a sad melancholy letter and prevented us all from sleeping.

Monday 7 December

We rose by candlelight. A showery unpleasant morning after a downright rainy night. We determined however to go to Keswick if possible, and we set off at a little after nine o'clock. When we were upon the Rays it snowed very much and the whole prospect closed in upon us like a moorland valley upon a moor—very wild—but when we were at the top of the Rays we saw the mountains before us. The sun shone upon them here and there and Wytheburn vale though wild looked soft. The rain went on cheerfully and pleasantly now and then a hail shower attacked us but we kept up a good heart for Mary is a famous jockey. We met Miss Barcroft—she had been unwell in the 'Liverpool complaint' and was riding out for the benefit of her health. She had not seen Mrs C. 'The weather had been such as to preclude all intercourse between neighbours!' We reached Greta Hall at about one o'clock. Met Mrs C. in the field. Derwent in the cradle asleep—Hartley at his dinner—Derwent pale, the image of his father, Hartley well. We wrote to C. Mrs C. left us at half past two—we drank tea by ourselves, the children playing about us. Mary said to Hartley, Shall I take Derwent with me? No says H. I cannot spare my little brother in the sweetest tone possible and he can't do without his Mama. Well says Mary, why cannot I be his Mama. Can't he have more Mamas than one? No says H. What for? Because they do not love as Mothers do. What is the difference between Mothers and Mamas? Looking at his sleeves, Mothers wear sleeves like this pulling his own tight down and Mamas (pulling them up and making a bustle about his shoulders) so—. We parted from them at four o'clock. It was a little of the dusk when we set off. Cotton mills lighted up. The first star at Nadel Fell, but it was never dark. We rode very briskly. Snow upon the Rays—reached home far sooner than we expected, at seven o'clock. William at work with Chaucer, 'The God of Love'. Sat latish. I wrote a little to C.

By John Harden

Tuesday 8 December

A dullish rainyish morning. Wm at work with Chaucer. I read Bruce's *Lochleven* and *Life*. Going to bake bread and pies. After dinner I felt myself unwell having not slept well in the night so, after we had put up the book cases which Charles Lloyd sent us I lay down. I did not sleep much but I rose refreshed. Mary and William walked to the boat

Windermere from Brathay Hall, by John Harden

house at Rydale while I was in bed. It rained very hard all night. No company. Wm worked at 'The Cuckoo and the Nightingale' till he was tired. Mary very sleepy and not quite well. We both slept sound. Letter from Rd with news of John dated 7th August.

Wednesday 9 December

William slept well but his tongue feverish. I read 'Palamon and Arcite'. Mary read Bruce. William writing out his alteration of Chaucer's 'Cuckoo and Nightingale'. After dinner it was agreed that we should walk, when I had finished a letter to C., part of which I had written in the morning by the kitchen fire while the mutton was roasting. William did not go with us but Mary and I walked into Easedale and backwards and forwards in that large field under George Rawnson's white cottage. We had intended gathering mosses and for that purpose we turned into the green lane behind the tailor's but it was too dark to see the mosses. The river came galloping past the church as fast as it could come and when we got into Easedale we saw Churnmilk Force like a broad stream of snow. At the little foot-bridge we stopped to look at the company of rivers which came hurrying down the vale this way and that; it was a valley of streams and islands, with that great waterfall at the head and lesser falls in different parts of the mountains coming down to these rivers. We could hear the sound of those lesser falls but we could not *see* them. We walked backwards and forwards till all distant objects except the white shape of the waterfall, and the lines of the mountains were gone. We had the crescent moon when we went out, and at our return there were a few stars that shone dimly, but it was a grey cloudy night.

Waterfall, by John White Abbott

Thursday 10 December

A very fine sunny morning—not frosty. We walked into Easedale to gather mosses, and then we went past to Aggy Fleming's and up the gill, beyond that little waterfall. It was a wild scene of crag and mountain. One craggy point rose above the rest irregular and ragged and very impressive it was. We called at Aggy Fleming's she told us about her miserable house. She looked shockingly with her head tied up. Her mother was there—the children looked healthy. We were very unsuccessful in our search after mosses. Just when the evening was closing in Mr Clarkson came to the door. It was a fine frosty evening. We played at cards.

Friday 11 December

Baked pies and cakes. It was a stormy morning with hail showers. The Luffs dined with us—Mrs L. came with Mrs Olliff in the gig. We sat lazily round the fire after dinner. Mr and Mrs Olliff drank tea and supped with us—a hard frost when they came.

Saturday 12 December

A fine frosty morning—snow upon the ground. I made bread and pies. We walked with Mrs Luff to Rydale, and came home on the other side of the lake. Met Townley with his dogs. All looked cheerful and bright. Helm Crag rose very bold and craggy, a being by itself, and behind it was the large ridge of mountain smooth as marble and snow white. All the mountains looked like solid stone on our left going from Grasmere, i.e. White Moss and Nab Scar. The snow hid all the grass and all signs of vegetation and the rocks showed themselves boldly everywhere and seemed more stony than rock or stone. The birches on the crags beautiful, red brown and glittering—the ashes glittering spears with their upright stems—the hips very beautiful, and so good!! and dear Coleridge—I ate twenty for thee when I was by myself. I came home first—they walked too slow for me. William went to look at Langdale Pikes. We had a sweet invigorating walk. Mr Clarkson came in before tea. We played at cards—sat up late. The moon shone upon the water below Silver How, and above it hung, combining with Silver How on one side, a bowl-shaped moon the curve downwards—the white fields, glittering roof of Thomas Ashburner's house, the dark yew tree, the white fields—gay and beautiful. William lay with his curtains open that he might see it.

Sunday 13 December

Mr Clarkson left us leading his horse. Went to Brathay to Luff's. We drank tea at Betty Dixon's. Very cold and frosty—a pleasant walk home. William had been very unwell but we found him better. The boy brought letters from Coleridge and from Sara. Sara in bad spirits about C.

Monday 14 December

Wm and Mary walked to Ambleside in the morning to buy mouse-traps. Mary fell and hurt her wrist. I accompanied them to the top of the hill—clear and frosty. I wrote to Coleridge, a very long letter while they were absent. Sat by the fire in the evening reading.

Tuesday 15 December

Wm and I walked to Rydale for letters—found one from Joanna. We had a pleasant walk but coldish—it thawed a little.

Wednesday 16 December

A very keen frost, extremely slippery. After dinner Wm and I walked twice up to The Swan and back again—met Miss Simpson. She came with us to Olliff's and we went back with her. Very cold.

Thusday 17 December

Snow in the night and still snowing. We went to Mr Luff's to dine—met Mrs King. Hard frost and as light as day—we had a delightful walk and reached home a little after twelve. Mrs Luff ill. Ambleside looked excessively beautiful as we came out—like a village in another country; and the light cheerful mountains were seen in the long long distance as bright and as clear as at midday with the blue sky above them. We heard waterfowl calling out by the lakeside. Jupiter was very glorious above the Ambleside hills and one large star hung over the coombe of the hills on the opposite side of Rydale water.

Friday 18 December

Mary and Wm walked round the two lakes. I stayed at home to make bread, cakes and pies. I went afterwards to meet them, and I met Wm near Benson's. Mary had gone to look at Langdale Pikes. It was a cheerful glorious day. The birches and all trees beautiful—hips bright red—mosses green. I wrote to Coleridge for money.

Saturday 19 December

I was not quite well and did not rise to breakfast. We walked by Brathay to Ambleside—called at the Lloyds'—they were at Kendal. Dined with the Luffs—and came home in the evening—the evening cloudy and promising snow. The day very beautiful—Brathay vale scattered and very cheerful and interesting.

Sunday 20 December

It snowed all day. In the evening we went to tea at Thomas Ashburner's. It was a very deep snow. The brooms were very beautiful, arched feathers with wiry stalks pointed to the end, smaller and smaller. They waved gently with the weight of the snow. We stayed at Thomas A.'s till after eight o'clock. Peggy better—the lasses neat and clean and rosy.

Monday 21 December

clapped: ironed

Being the shortest day. Mary walked to Ambleside for letters, it was a wearisome walk for the snow lay deep upon the roads and it was beginning to thaw. I stayed at home and clapped the small linen. Wm sat beside me and read 'The Pedlar', he was in good spirits, and full of hope of what he should do with it. He went to meet Mary and they brought four letters, two from Coleridge, one from Sara and one from France. Coleridge's were very melancholy letters, he had been very ill in his bowels. We were made very unhappy. Wm wrote to him and directed the letter into Somersetshire. I finished it after tea. In the afternoon Mary and I ironed—afterwards she packed her clothes up and I mended Wm's stockings while he was reading 'The Pedlar'. I then packed up for Mr Clarkson's—we carried the boxes cross the road to Fletcher's peat house, after Mary had written to Sara and Joanna.

Waterfall, by Sir William Gell

Tuesday 22 December

Still thaw. I washed my head. Wm and I went to Rydale for letters. The road was covered with dirty snow, rough and rather slippery. We had a melancholy letter from C., for he had been very ill, though he was better when he wrote. We walked home almost without speaking. Wm composed a few lines of 'The Pedlar'. We talked about Lamb's Tragedy as we went down the White Moss. We stopped a long time in going to watch a little bird with a salmon coloured breast—a white cross or T upon its wings, and a brownish back with faint stripes. It was pecking the scattered dung upon the road. It began to peck at the distance of four yards from us and advanced nearer and nearer till it came within the length of Wm's stick without any apparent fear of us. As we came up the White Moss we met an old man who I saw was a beggar by his two bags hanging over his shoulder, but from a half laziness, half indifference and a wanting to *try* him if he would speak I let him pass. He said nothing, and my heart smote me. I turned back and said You are begging? 'Ay,' says he. I gave him a halfpenny. William, judging from his appearance joined in I suppose you were a sailor? 'Ay,' he replied, 'I have been 57 years at sea, twelve of them on board a man-of-war under Sir Hugh Palmer.' Why have you not a pension? 'I have no pension, but I could have got into Greenwich hospital but all my officers are dead.' He was 75 years of age, had freshish colour in his cheeks, grey hair, a decent hat with a binding round the edge, the hat worn brown and glossy, *his* shoes were small thin shoes low in the quarters, pretty good. They had belonged to a gentleman. His coat was blue, frock shaped coming over his thighs, it had been joined up at the seams behind with paler blue to let it out, and there were three bell-shaped patches of darker blue behind where the buttons had been. His breeches were either of fustian or grey cloth, with strings hanging down, whole and tight; he had a checked shirt on, and a small coloured handkerchief tied round his neck. His bags were hung over each shoulder and lay on each side of him, below his breast. One was brownish and of coarse stuff, the other was white with meal on the outside, and his blue waistcoat was whitened with meal. In the coarse bag I guessed he put his scraps of meat etc. He walked with a slender stick decently stout, but his legs bowed outwards. We overtook old Fleming at Rydale, leading his little Dutchman-like grandchild along the slippery road. The same pace seemed to be natural to them both, the old man and the little child, and they went hand in hand, the grandfather cautious, yet looking proud of his charge. He had two patches of new cloth at the shoulder blades of his faded claret coloured coat, like eyes at each shoulder, not worn elsewhere. I found Mary at home in her riding-habit all her clothes being put up. We were very sad about Coleridge. Wm walked further. When he came home he cleared a path to the necessary—called me out to see it but before we got there a whole housetop full of snow had fallen from the roof upon the path and it echoed in the ground beneath like a dull beating upon it. We talked of going to Ambleside after dinner to borrow money of Luff, but we thought we would defer our visit to Eusemere a day.—Half the seaman's nose was reddish as if he had been in his youth somewhat used to drinking, though he was not injured by it.—We stopped to look at the stone seat at the top of the hill. There was a white cushion upon it round at the edge like a cushion and the rock behind looked soft as velvet, of a vivid green and so tempting! The snow too looked as soft as a down cushion. A young foxglove, like a star in the centre. There were a few green lichens about it and a few withered brackens of fern here and there and upon the ground near. All else was a thick snow—no foot mark to it, not the foot of a sheep.—When we were at Thomas Ashburner's on Sunday Peggy talked about the Queen of Patterdale.

The Queen of Patterdale, wife of the famed eccentric John Mounsey,
by John White Abbott

She had been brought to drinking by her husband's unkindness and avarice. She was formerly a very nice tidy woman. She had taken to drinking but 'that was better than if she had taken to something worse' (by this I suppose she meant killing herself). She said that her husband used to be out all night with other women and she used to *hear* him come in in the morning for they never slept together—'Many a poor body a wife like me, has had a working heart for her, as much stuff as she had.' We sat snugly round the fire. I read to them 'The Tale of Custance and the Syrian Monarch', also some of the Prologues. It is 'The Man of Law's Tale'. We went to bed early. It snowed and thawed.

Wednesday 23 December

A downright thaw but the snow not gone off the ground except on the steep hillsides—it was a thick black heavy air. I baked pies and bread. Mary wrote out the Tales from Chaucer for Coleridge. William worked at 'The Ruined Cottage' and made himself very ill. I went to bed without dinner, he went to the other bed—we both slept and Mary lay on the rug before the fire. A broken soldier came to beg in the morning. Afterwards a tall woman, dressed somewhat in a tawdry style with a long checked muslin apron a beaver hat, and throughout what are called *good clothes*. Her daughter had gone before with a soldier and his wife. She had buried her husband at Whitehaven and was going back into Cheshire.

Thursday 24 December

Still a thaw. We walked to Rydale, Wm Mary and I—left the patterns at Thomas Fleming's for Mrs King. The roads uncomfortable and slippery. We sat comfortably round the fire in the evening and read Chaucer. Thoughts of last year. I took out my old journal.

By John Harden

Friday 25 December, Christmas Day

A very bad day. We drank tea at John Fisher's—we were unable to walk. I went to bed after dinner. The roads very slippery. We received a letter from Coleridge while we were at John Fisher's. A terrible night—little John brought the letter. Coleridge poorly but better—his letter made us uneasy about him. I was glad I was not by myself when I received it.

Saturday 26 December

My head ached and I lay long in bed and took my breakfast there. Soon after I had breakfasted we went to call at Mr Olliff's. They were not at home. It came on very wet. Mary went in to the house, and Wm and I went up to Tom Dawson's to speak about his grandchild. The rain went off and we walked to Rydale. It was very pleasant—Grasmere lake a beautiful image of stillness, clear as glass, reflecting all things. The wind was up and the waters sounding. The lake of a rich purple, the fields a soft yellow, the island yellowish-green, the copses red brown the mountains purple. The church and buildings, how quiet they were! Poor Coleridge, Sara, and dear little Derwent here last year at this

Grasmere, by Henry Gastineau

time. After tea we sat by the fire comfortably. I read aloud—'The Miller's Tale'. Wrote to Coleridge. The Olliffs passed in chaise and gig. Wm wrote part of the poem to Coleridge.

Sunday 27 December

A fine soft beautiful, mild day with gleams of sunshine. I lay in bed till twelve o'clock, Mr Clarkson's man came. We wrote to him. We walked up within view of Rydale. William went to take in his boat. I sat in John's Grove a little while. Mary came home. Mary wrote some lines of the third part of Wm's poem which he brought to read to us when we came home. Mr Simpson came in at dinner time and stayed tea. They fetched in the boat. I lay down upon the bed in the mean time. A sweet evening.

Monday 28 December

William, Mary and I set off on foot to Keswick. We carried some cold mutton in our pockets, and dined at John Stanley's where they were making Christmas pies. The sun shone but it was coldish. We parted from Wm upon the Rays. He joined us opposite Sara's rock. He was busy in composition and sat down upon the wall. We did not see him again till we arrived at John Stanley's. There we roasted apples in the oven. After we had left John Stanley's Wm discovered that he had lost his gloves. He turned back but they were gone. We were tired and had bad headaches. We rested often. Once Wm left his spencer and Mary turned back for it and found it upon the bank where we had last rested. *spencer:* jacket We reached Greta Hall at about half past five o'clock. The children and Mrs C. well. After tea message came from Wilkinson who had passed us on the road inviting Wm to sup at The Oak. He went. Met a young man (a predestined Marquis) called Johnston. He spoke to him familiarly of the *Lyrical Ballads*. He had seen a copy presented by the Queen to Mrs Harcourt. Said he saw them everywhere and wondered they did not sell. We all went weary to bed. My bowels very bad.

Tuesday 29 December

A fine morning. A thin fog upon the hills which soon disappeared. The sun shone. Wilkinson went with us to the top of the hill. We turned out of the road at the second milestone and passed a pretty cluster of houses at the foot of St John's Vale. The houses were among tall trees partly of Scotch fir, and some naked forest trees. We crossed a bridge just below these houses and the river winded sweetly along the meadows. Our road soon led us along the sides of dreary bare hills, but we had a glorious prospect to the left of Saddleback, half way covered with snow and underneath the comfortable white houses and the village of Threlkeld. These houses and the village want trees about them. Skiddaw was behind us and dear Coleridge's desert home— —As we ascended the hills it grew very cold and slippery. Luckily the wind was at our backs and helped us on. A sharp hail shower gathered at the head of Matterdale and the view upwards was very grand— the wild cottages seen through the hurrying hail shower. The wind drove and eddied about and about the hills looked large and swelling through the storm. We thought of Coleridge. O the bonny nooks and windings and curlings of the beck down at the bottom of the steep green mossy banks. We dined at the public house on porridge, with a second course of Christmas pies. We were well received by the landlady, and her little Jewish

daughters were glad to see us again. The husband a very handsome man. While we were eating our dinners a traveller came in. He had walked over Kirkstone that morning. We were much amused by the curiosity of the landlord and landlady to learn who he was, and by his mysterious manner of letting out a little bit of his errand and yet telling nothing. He had business further up in the vale. He left them with this piece of information to work upon and I doubt not they discovered who he was and all his business before the next day at that hour. The woman told us of the riches of a Mr Walker formerly of Grasmere. We said What does he do nothing for his relations? He has a sickly sister at Grasmere. 'Why,' said the man, 'I daresay if they had any sons to put forward he would do it for them, but he has children of his own.' N.B.—his fortune is above sixty thousand pounds and he has two children!! The landlord went about a mile and a half with us to put us in the right way. The road was often very slippery, the wind high, and it was nearly dark before we got into the right road. I was often obliged to crawl upon all fours, and Mary fell many a time. A stout young man whom we met on the hills and who knew Mr Clarkson very kindly set us into the right road and we inquired again near some houses and were directed by a miserable poverty struck looking woman, who had been fetching water, to go down a nasty miry lane. We soon got into the main road and reached Mr Clarkson's at tea time. Mary H. spent the next day with us and we walked in Dunmallet before dinner but it snowed a little. The day following being New Year's Eve we accompanied Mary to Stainton Bridge—met Mr Clarkson with a calf's head in a basket—we turned with him and parted from Mary.

Saddleback and part of Skiddaw, by John Constable

· *1802* ·

New Year's Day

We walked Wm and I towards Martindale.

Saturday 2 January

It snowed all day. We walked near to Dalemain in the snow.

Sunday 3 January

Mary brought us letters from Sara and Coleridge and we went with her homewards to Sockbridge. Parted at the style on the Poolley side. Thomas Wilkinson dined with us, and stayed supper.

I do not recollect how the rest of our time was spent exactly. We had a very sharp frost which broke on Friday the 15th January, or rather on the morning of Saturday 16th.—
—On Sunday the 17th we went to meet Mary—it was a mild gentle thaw. She stayed with us till Friday 22nd January—she was to have left us on Thursday 21st but it was too stormy. On Thursday we dined at Mr Myers's and on Friday 22nd, we parted from Mary. Before our parting we sat under a wall in the sun near a cottage above Stainton Bridge. The field in which we sat sloped downwards to a nearly level meadow round which the Emont flowed in a small half circle, as at Sockburn. The opposite bank is woody, steep as a wall, but not high, and above that bank the fields slope gently and irregularly down to it. These fields are surrounded by tall hedges with trees among them, and there are *clumps* or grovelets of tall trees here and there. Sheep and cattle were in the fields. Dear Mary! there we parted from her. I daresay, as often as she passes that road she will turn in at the gate to look at this sweet prospect. There was a barn and I think two or three cottages to be seen among the trees and slips of lawn and irregular fields. During our stay at Mr Clarkson's we walked every day, except that stormy Thursday and then Wm dined at Mr Myers's and I went after dinner on a double horse. Mrs Clarkson was poorly all the time we were there. We dined at Thomas Wilkinson's on Friday the 15th and walked to Penrith for Mary. The trees were covered with hoarfrost, grasses and trees and hedges beautiful—a glorious sunset frost keener than ever. Next day thaw. Mrs Clarkson amused us with many stories of her family and of persons whom she had known. I wish I had set them down as I heard them, when they were fresh in my memory. She had two old aunts who lived at Norwich. The son of one of them (Mrs Barnard) had had a large fortune left him. The other sister rather piqued that her child had not got it says to her, 'Well, we have one squire in the family however.' Mrs Barnard

replied with tears rushing out, 'Sister Harmer Sister Harmer there you sit. My son's no more a squire than yours. I take it very unkindly of you Sister Harmer.' She used to say, 'Well I wish it may do him any good.' When her son wished to send his carriage for her she said, 'Nay I can walk to the tabernacle and surely I may walk to see him.' She kept two maids yet she white-washed her kitchen herself—the two sisters lived together. She had a grand cleaning day twice a week and the sister had a fire made upstairs that all below might be thoroughly cleaned. She gave a great deal away in charity, visited the sick and was very pious. Mrs Clarkson knew a clergyman and his wife who brought up ten children upon a curacy, sent two sons to college, and he left a thousand pounds when he died. The wife was very generous gave to all poor people victuals and drink. She had a passion for feeding animals, she killed a pig with feeding it over much. When it was dead she said, 'To be sure it's a great loss but I thank God it did not die *clemmed*', the Cheshire word for starved. Her husband was very fond of playing backgammon and used to play whenever he could get anybody to play with him. She had played much in her youth and was an excellent player but her husband knew nothing of this, till one day she said to him, 'You're fond of backgammon come play with me.' He was surprised. She told him that she had kept it to herself while she had a young family to attend to but that now she would play with him. So they began to play and played afterwards every night. Mr C. told us many pleasant stories. His journey from London to Wisbech on foot when a schoolboy, Irish murderer's knife and stick, postboy, &c., the white horse sleeping at the turnpike gate, snoring of the turnpike man, clock ticking. The burring story, the story of the mastiff, bull-baitings by men at Wisbech. On Saturday January 23rd we left Eusemere at ten o'clock in the morning, I behind Wm Mr C. on his Galloway. The

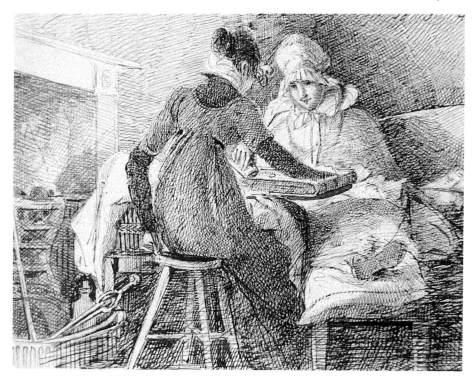

A game of backgammon, by John Harden

View in Borrowdale, by John Constable

morning not very promising the wind cold. The mountains large and dark but only thinly streaked with snow—a strong wind. We dined in Grisedale on ham bread and milk. We parted from Mr C. at one o'clock—it rained all the way home. We struggled with the wind and often rested as we went along.—A hail shower met us before we reached the tarn and the way often was difficult over the snow but at the tarn the view closed in. We saw nothing but mists and snow and at first the ice on the tarn below us, cracked and split yet without water, a dull grey white. We lost our path and could see the tarn no longer. We made our way out with difficulty guided by a heap of stones which we well remembered. We were afraid of being bewildered in the mists till the darkness should overtake us. We were long before we knew that we were in the right track but thanks to William's skill we knew it long before we could see our way before us. There was no footmark upon the snow either of man or beast. We saw four sheep before we had left the snow region. The vale of Grasmere when the mists broke away looked soft and grave, of a yellow hue—it was dark before we reached home. We were not very much tired. My inside was sore with the cold. We had both of us been much heated upon the mountains but we caught no cold— —O how comfortable and happy we felt ourselves sitting by our own fire when we had got off our wet clothes and had dressed ourselves fresh and clean. We found five pounds from Montague and twenty pounds from Christopher. We talked about the Lake of Como, read in the descriptive sketches, looked about us, and felt that we were happy. We indulged all dear thoughts about home—poor Mary! we were sad to think of the contrast for her.

Sunday 24 January

We went into the orchard as soon as breakfast was over laid out the situation for our new room, and sauntered a while. We had Mr Clarkson's turkey for dinner, the night before we had broiled the gizzard and some mutton and made a nice piece of cookery for Wm's supper. Wm walked in the morning I wrote to Coleridge. After dinner I lay down till tea time. I rose fresher and better. Wm could not beat away sleep when I was gone. We went late to bed.

Monday 25 January

We did not rise as soon as we intended. I made bread and apple pies. We walked at dusk to

Rydale—no letters! it rained all the way. I wrote to Christopher and Mrs Clarkson and Mrs Coleridge, and sent off C.'s letter to Mary. William tired with composition. We both went to bed at ten o'clock.

Tuesday 26 January

A dull morning. I have employed myself in writing this journal and reading newspapers till now (half past one o'clock) we are going to walk, and I am ready and waiting by the kitchen fire for Wm. We set forward, intending to go into Easedale but the wind being rather loudish, and blowing down Easedale we turned under Silver How for a sheltered walk. We went a little beyond the Wyke then up to John's Grove, where the storm of Thursday has made sad ravages. Two of the finest trees are uprooted one lying with the turf about its root as if the whole together had been pared by a knife. The other is a larch. Several others are blown aside, one is snapped in two. We gathered together a faggot. William had tired himself with working—he resolved to do better. We received a letter from Mary by Fletcher with an account of C.'s arrival in London. I wrote to Mary before bed-time. We sat till we were both tired, for Wm wrote out part of his poem and endeavoured to alter it, and so made himself ill. I copied out the rest for him. We went late to bed. Wm wrote to Annette.

Wednesday 27 January

A beautiful mild morning—the sun shone, the lake was still, and all the shores reflected in it. I finished my letter to Mary, Wm wrote to Stuart. I copied out sonnets for him. Mr Olliff called and asked us to tea tomorrow. We stayed in the house till the sun shone more dimly and we thought the afternoon was closing in but, though the calmness of the lake was gone with the bright sunshine, yet it was delightfully pleasant. We found no letter from Coleridge. One from Sara which we sat upon the wall to read—a sweet long

Grasmere, by John Harden

letter, with a most interesting account of Mr Patrick. We had ate up the cold turkey before we walked so we cooked no dinner. Sat a while by the fire and then drank tea at Frank Baty's. As we went past the Nab, I was surprised to see the youngest child amongst the rest of them running about by itself with a canny round fat face, and rosy cheeks. I called in. They gave me some nuts—everybody surprised that we should both come over Grisedale. Paid one pound three and threepence for letters come since December 1st. Paid also about eight shillings at Penrith. The bees were humming about the hive. William raked a few stones off the garden, his first garden labour this year. I cut the shrubs. When we returned from Frank's William wasted his mind in the magazines. I wrote to Coleridge and Mrs C., closed the letters up to Ianson. Then we sat by the fire and were happy only our tender thoughts became painful. Went to bed at half past eleven.

Thursday 28 January

A downright rain. A wet night. Wm slept better—better this morning—he had written an epitaph and altered one that he wrote when he was a boy. It cleared up after dinner. We were both in miserable spirits, and very doubtful about keeping our engagement to the Olliffs. We walked first within view of Rydale, then to Lewthwaite's, then we went to Mr Olliff's. We talked a while. William was tired. We then played at cards. Came home in the rain. Very dark. Came with a lantern. William out of spirits and tired. After we went to bed I heard him continually, he called at quarter past three to know the hour.

Friday 29 January

William was very unwell. Worn out with his bad night's rest—he went to bed—I read to him to endeavour to make him sleep. Then I came into the other room, and read the first

Figures round a blazing fire, by William Payne

book of *Paradise Lost*. After dinner we walked to Ambleside. Found Lloyds at Luff's—we stayed and drank tea by ourselves. A heart-rending letter from Coleridge—we were sad as we could be. Wm wrote to him. We talked about Wm's going to London. It was a mild afternoon—there was an unusual softness in the prospects as we went, a rich yellow upon the fields, and a soft grave purple on the waters. When we returned, many stars were out, the clouds were moveless, in the sky soft purple, the lake of Rydale calm, Jupiter behind, Jupiter at least *we* call him, but William says we always call the largest star Jupiter. When we came home we both wrote to C. I was stupefied.

Saturday 30 January

A cold dark morning. William chopped wood—I brought it in a basket. A cold wind. Wm slept better but he thinks he looks ill—he is shaving now. He asks me to set down the story of Barbara Wilkinson's turtle dove. Barbara is an old maid. She had two turtle doves. One of them died the first year I think. The other bird continued to live alone in its cage for nine years, but for one whole year it had a companion and daily visitor, a little mouse that used to come and feed with it, and the dove would caress it, and cower over it with its wings, and make a loving noise to it. The mouse though it did not testify equal delight in the dove's company yet it was at perfect ease. The poor mouse disappeared and the dove was left solitary till its death. It died of a short sickness and was buried under a tree with funeral ceremony by Barbara and her maiden, and one or two others.

On Saturday 30th, William worked at 'The Pedlar' all the morning. He kept the dinner waiting till four o'clock—he was much tired. We were preparing to walk when a heavy rain came on.

Sunday 31 January

William had slept very ill—he was tired and had a bad headache. We walked round the two lakes. Grasmere was very soft and Rydale was extremely beautiful from the pasture side. Nab Scar was just topped by a cloud which cutting it off as high as it could be cut off made the mountain look uncommonly lofty. We sat down a long time in different places. I always love to walk that way because it is the way I first came to Rydale and Grasmere, and because our dear Coleridge did also. When I came with Wm six and a half years ago it was just at sunset. There was a rich yellow light on the waters and the islands were reflected there. Today it was grave and soft but not perfectly calm. William says it was much such a day as when Coleridge came with him. The sun shone out before we reached Grasmere. We sat by the roadside at the foot of the lake close to Mary's dear name which she had cut herself upon the stone. William cut at it with his knife to make it plainer. We amused ourselves for a long time in watching the breezes some as if they came from the bottom of the lake spread in a circle, brushing along the surface of the water, and growing more delicate, as it were thinner and of a *paler* colour till they died away. Others spread out like a peacock's tail, and some went right forward this way and that in all directions. The lake was still where these breezes were not, but they made it all alive. I found a strawberry blossom in a rock. The little slender flower had more courage than the green leaves, for *they* were but half expanded and half grown, but the blossom was spread full out. I uprooted it rashly, and I felt as if I had been committing an outrage, so I planted it again. It will have but a stormy life of it, but let it live if it can. We found Calvert here. I brought a handerchief full of mosses which I placed on the chimneypiece when C. was gone. He dined with us and carried away the Encyclopaedias. After they were gone I

Mosses,
by John Ruskin

spent some time in trying to reconcile myself to the change, and in rummaging out and arranging some other books in their places. One good thing is this—there is a nice elbow place for William, and he may sit for the picture of John Bunyan any day. Mr Simpson drank tea with us. We paid our rent to Benson. William's head bad after Mr S. was gone. I petted him on the carpet and began a letter to Sara.

Monday 1 February

Wm slept badly. I baked pies and bread. William worked hard at 'The Pedlar' and tired himself. He walked up with me towards Mr Simpson's. There was a purplish light upon Mr Olliff's house which made me look to the other side of the vale when I saw a strange stormy mist coming down the side of Silver How of reddish purple colour. It soon came on a heavy rain. We parted presently. Wm went to Rydale—I drank tea with Mrs S. The two Mr Simpsons both tipsy. I came home with Jenny as far as The Swan—a cold night, dry and windy—Jupiter above the forest side. Wm pretty well but he worked a little. In the morning a box of clothes with books came from London. I sat by his bedside, and read in the *Pleasures of Hope* to him, which came in the box. He could not fall asleep, but I found in the morning that he had slept better than he expected. No letters.

Tuesday 2 February

A fine clear morning but sharp and cold. William went into the orchard after breakfast to chop wood. I walked backwards and forwards on the platform. Molly called me down to Charles Lloyd, he brought me flower seeds from his brother. William not quite well. We walked into Easedale—were turned back in the open field by the sight of a cow. Every horned cow puts me in terror. We walked as far as we could having crossed the foot-bridge, but it was dirty, and we turned back—walked backwards and forwards between Goody Bridge and Butterlip How. William wished to break off composition, and was unable, and so did himself harm. The sun shone but it was cold. After dinner Wm worked at 'The Pedlar'. After tea I read aloud the eleventh book of *Paradise Lost*. We were much impressed and also melted into tears. The papers came in soon after I had laid aside the book—a good thing for my William. I worked a little today at putting the linen into repair that came in the box. Molly washing.

Wednesday 3 February

A rainy morning. We walked to Rydale for letters, found one from Mrs Cookson and Mary H. It snowed upon the hills. We sat down on the wall at the foot of White Moss. Sat by the fire in the evening. William tired and did not compose. He went to bed soon and could not sleep. I wrote to Mary H., sent off the letter by Fletcher. Wrote also to Coleridge—read Wm to sleep after dinner, and read to him in bed till half past one.

Thursday 4 February

I was very sick, bad headache and unwell—I lay in bed till three o'clock that is I lay down as soon as breakfast was over. It was a terribly wet day. William sat in the house all day. Fletcher's boy did not come home. I worked at Montagu's shirts. Wm thought a little about 'The Pedlar'. I slept in the sitting room. Read Smollett's life.

Grasmere from Butter Crags, by Thomas Allom

Friday 5 February

A cold snowy morning. Snow and hail showers. We did not walk. William cut wood a little. I read the story of Snell in *Wanly Penson*. Sara's parcel came with waistcoat. The Chaucer not only misbound but a leaf or two wanting. I wrote about it to Mary and wrote to Soulby. We received the waistcoats, shoes and gloves from *Sara* by the waggon. William not well. Sat up late at 'The Pedlar'.

Saturday 6 February

William had slept badly. It snowed in the night, and was, on Saturday, as Molly expressed it, a Cauld Clash. William went to Rydale for letters, he came home with two very affecting letters from Coleridge—resolved to try another climate. I was stopped in my writing, and made ill by the letters. William a bad headache; he made up a bed on the floor, but could not sleep—I went to his bed and slept not—better when I rose. Wrote again after tea and translated two or three of Lessing's fables.

Sunday 7 February

A fine clear frosty morning. The eaves drop with the heat of the sun all day long. The ground thinly covered with snow. The road black, rocks bluish. Before night the island was quite green, the sun had melted all the snow upon it. Mr Simpson called before William had done shaving—William had had a bad night and was working at his poem. We sat by the fire and did not walk, but read 'The Pedlar' thinking it done but lo, though Wm could find fault with no one part of it—it was uninteresting and must be altered. Poor William.

Cottage interior, by John Harden

Monday 8 February

It was very windy and rained very hard all the morning. William worked at his poem and I read a little in Lessing and the grammar. A chaise came past to fetch Ellis the carrier who had hurt his head. After dinner (i.e. we set off at about half past four) we went towards Rydale for letters. It was a cold 'Cauld Clash'. The rain had been so cold that it hardly melted the snow. We stopped at Park's to get some straw in William's shoes. The young mother was sitting by a bright wood fire with her youngest child upon her lap and the other two sat on each side of the chimney. The light of the fire made them a beautiful sight, with their innocent countenances, their rosy cheeks and glossy curling hair. We sat and talked about poor Ellis, and our journey over the Hawes. It had been reported that we came over in the night. Willy told us of three men who were once lost in crossing that way in the night, they had carried a lantern with them—the lantern went out at the tarn and they all perished. Willy had seen their cloaks drying at the public house in Patterdale the day before their funeral. We walked on very wet through the clashy cold roads in bad spirits at the idea of having to go as far as Rydale, but before we had come again to the shore of the lake, we met our patient, bow-bent friend with his little wooden box at his back. 'Where are you going?' said he. 'To Rydale for letters.' 'I have two for you in my box.' We lifted up the lid and there they lay. Poor fellow, he straddled and pushed on with all his might but we soon outstripped him far away when we had turned back with our letters. We were very thankful that we had not to go on, for we should have been sadly tired. In thinking of this I could not help comparing lots with him! He goes at that slow pace every morning, and after having wrought a hard day's work returns at night, however weary he may be, takes it all quietly, and though perhaps he neither feels thankfulness, nor pleasure when he eats his supper, and has no luxury to look forward to but falling asleep in bed, yet I daresay he neither murmurs nor thinks it hard. He seems mechanized to labour. We broke the seal of Coleridge's letter, and I had light enough just to see that he was not ill. I put it in my pocket but at the top of the White Moss I took it to my bosom, a safer place for it. The night was wild. There was a strange mountain lightness when we were at the top of the White Moss. I have often observed it there in the evenings, being between the two valleys. There is more of the sky there than any other place. It has a strange effect sometimes along with the obscurity of evening or night. It seems almost like a peculiar *sort* of light. There was not much wind till we came to John's Grove, then it roared right out of the grove, all the trees were tossing about. C.'s letter somewhat damped us, it spoke with less confidence about France. William wrote to him. The other letter was from Montagu with eight pounds. William was very unwell, tired when he had written he went to bed, and left me to write to M. H., Montagu and Calvert, and Mrs Coleridge. I had written in his letter to Coleridge. We wrote to Calvert to beg him not to fetch us on Sunday. Wm left me with a *little* peat fire—it grew less. I wrote on and was starved. At two o'clock I went to put my letters under Fletcher's door. I never felt *starved:* cold such a cold night. There was a strong wind and it froze very hard. I collected together all the clothes I could find (for I durst not go into the pantry for fear of waking William). At first when I went to bed I seemed to be warm, I suppose because the cold air, which I had just left, no longer touched my body, but I soon found that I was mistaken. I could not sleep from sheer cold. I had baked pies and bread in the morning. Coleridge's letter contained prescriptions. N.B. The moon came out suddenly when we were at John's Grove, and 'a star or two beside'.

Tuesday 9 February

William had slept better. He fell to work, and made himself unwell. We did not walk. A funeral came by of a poor woman who had drowned herself, some say because she was hardly treated by her husband, others that he was a very decent respectable man and *she* but an indifferent wife. However this was she had only been married to him last Whitsuntide and had had very indifferent health ever since. She had got up in the night and drowned herself in the pond. She had requested to be buried beside her mother and so she was brought in a hearse. She was followed by several decent-looking men on horseback, her sister, Thomas Fleming's wife, in a chaise, and some others with her, and a cart full of women. Molly says folks thinks o' their mothers. Poor body *she* has been little thought of by anybody else. We did a little of Lessing. I attempted a fable, but my head ached my bones were sore with the cold of the day before and I was downright stupid. We went to bed but not till William had tired himself.

Wednesday 10 February

A very snowy morning. It cleared up a little however for a while but we did not walk. We sent for our letters by Fletcher and for some writing paper etc. He brought us word there were none. This was strange for I depended upon Mary. While I was writing out the poem as we hope for a final writing, a letter was brought me by John Dawson's daughter, the letter written at Eusemere.—I paid Wm Jackson's bill by John Fisher. Sent off a letter to Montagu by Fletcher. After Molly went we read the first part of the poem and were

Hawkshead and Esthwaite, from the north, by John Harden

delighted with it, but Wm afterwards got to some ugly places and went to bed tired out. A wild, moonlight night.

Thursday 11 February

A very fine clear sunny frost the ground white with snow—William rose before Molly was ready for him, I rose at a little after nine. William sadly tired and working still at 'The Pedlar'. Miss Simpson called when he was worn out—he escaped and sat in his own room till she went. She was very faint and ill, had had a tooth drawn and had suffered greatly. I walked up with her past Goan's. The sun was very warm till we got past Lewthwaite's—then it had little power, and had not melted the roads. As I came back again I felt the vale like a different climate. The vale was bright and beautiful. Molly had linen hung out. We had pork to dinner sent us by Mrs Simpson. William still poorly. We made up a good fire after dinner, and William brought his mattress out, and lay down on the floor. I read to him the life of Ben Jonson and some short poems of his which were too *interesting* for him, and would not let him go to sleep. I had begun with Fletcher, but he was too *dull* for me. Fuller says in his life of Jonson (speaking of his plays), 'If his latter be not so spriteful and vigorous as his first pieces all that are old, and all who desire to be old, should excuse him therein.' He says he had '*beheld*' wit combats between Shakespeare and Jonson, and compares Shakespeare to an English man of war, Jonson to a Spanish great galleon. There is one affecting line in Jonson's epitaph on his first daughter

> Here lies to each her parents' ruth,
> *Mary the daughter of their youth*
> At six months' end she parted hence
> In safety of her innocence.

I have been writing this journal while Wm has had a nice little sleep. Once he was waked by Charles Lloyd who had come to see about lodgings for his children in the whooping cough. It is now seven o'clock—I have a nice coal fire—Wm is still on his bed. Two beggars today. I continued to read to him. We were much delighted with the poem of 'Penshurst'. William rose better. I was cheerful and happy but he got to work again and went to bed unwell.

Friday 12 February

A very fine bright, clear, hard frost. William working again. I recopied 'The Pedlar', but poor William all the time at work. Molly tells me, 'What! little Sally's gone to visit at Mr Simpson's. They say she's very smart she's got on a new bed-gown that her cousin gave her. It's a very bonny one they tell me, but I've not seen it. Sally and me's in luck.' In the afternoon a poor woman came, *she said* to beg some rags for her husband's leg which had been wounded by a slate from the roof in the great wind—but she has been used to go a-begging, for she has often come here. Her father lived to the age of 105. She is a woman of strong bones with a complexion that has been beautiful, and remained very fresh last year, but now she looks broken, and her little boy, a pretty little fellow, and whom I have loved for the sake of Basil, looks thin and pale. I observed this to her. Aye says she we have all been ill. Our house was unroofed in the storm nearly and *so* we lived in it for more than a week. The child wears a ragged drab coat and a fur cap, poor little fellow, I think he seems scarcely at all grown since the first time I saw him. William was with me—we met him in a lane going to Skelwith Bridge. He looked very pretty. He was walking lazily in the deep narrow lane, overshadowed with the hedgerows, his meal poke hung over his shoulder. He said he was going 'a laiting'. He now wears the same coat he had on at that time. Poor creatures! When the woman was gone, I could not help thinking that we are not half thankful enough that we are placed in that condition of life in which we are. We do not so often bless God for this as we wish for this fifty pounds that hundred pounds etc. etc. We have not, however to reproach ourselves with ever breathing a murmur. This woman's was but a *common* case.—The snow still lies upon the ground. Just at the closing in of the day I heard a cart pass the door, and at the same time the dismal sound of a crying infant. I went to the window and had light enough to see that a man was driving a cart which seemed not to be very full, and that a woman with an infant in her arms was following close behind and a dog close to her. It was a wild and melancholy sight.—William rubbed his table after candles were lighted, and we sat a

Itinerants, by John Harden

long time with the windows unclosed. I almost finished writing 'The Pedlar', but poor William wore himself and me out with labour. We had an affecting conversation. Went to bed at twelve o'clock.

Saturday 13 February

It snowed a little this morning—still at work at 'The Pedlar', altering and refitting. We did not walk though it was a very fine day. We received a present of eggs and milk from Janet Dockeray, and just before she went the little boy from the hill brought us a letter from Sara H., and one from the Frenchman in London. I wrote to Sara after tea and Wm took out his old newspapers, and the new ones came in soon after. We sat, after I had finished the letter, talking and William read parts of his 'Recluse' aloud to me. We did not drink tea till half past seven.

Sunday 14 February

A fine morning. The sun shines but it has been a hard frost in the night. There are some little snowdrops that are afraid to pop their white heads quite out, and a few blossoms of hepatica that are half starved. William left me at work altering some passages of 'The Pedlar', and went into the orchard. The fine day pushed him on to resolve and as soon as I had read a letter to him which I had just received from Mrs Clarkson he said he would go to Penrith, so Molly was dispatched for the horse. I worked hard, got the backs pasted the writing finished, and all quite trim. I wrote to Mrs Clarkson and put up some letters for Mary H., and off he went in his blue spencer and a pair of *new* pantaloons fresh from London. He turned back when he had got as far as Frank's to ask if he had his letters safe, then for some apples—then fairly off. We had money to borrow for him.—It was a pleasant afternoon. I ate a little bit of cold mutton without laying cloth and then sat over the fire reading Ben Jonson's 'Penshurst', and other things. Before sunset I put on my shawl and walked out. The snow-covered mountains were spotted with rich sunlight, a palish buffish colour. The roads were very dirty, for though it was a keen frost the sun had melted the snow and water upon them. I stood at Sara's Gate and when I came in view of Rydale I cast a long look upon the mountains beyond. They were very white but I concluded that Wm would have a very safe passage over Kirkstone, and I was quite easy about him.

About twenty yards above Glowworm Rock I met a carman, a Highlander I suppose, with four carts, the first three belonging to himself, the last evidently to a man and his family who had joined company with him and who I guessed to be potters. The carman was cheering his horses and talking to a little lass about ten years of age who seemed to make him her companion. She ran to the wall and took up a large stone to support the wheel of one of his carts and ran on before with it in her arms to be ready for him. She was a beautiful creature and there was something uncommonly impressive in the lightness and joyousness of her manner. Her business seemed to be all pleasure— pleasure in her own motions—and the man looked at her as if he too was pleased and spoke to her in the same tone in which he spoke to his horses. There was a wildness in her whole figure, not the wildness of a mountain lass but a *road* lass, a traveller from her birth, who had wanted neither food nor clothes. Her mother followed the last cart with a lovely child, perhaps about a year old, at her back and a good-looking girl about fifteen years old walked beside her. All the children were like the mother. She had a very fresh complexion, but she was blown with fagging up the hill with the steepness of the hill and

Kirkstone between Ullswater and Ambleside, by John Glover

the bairn that she carried. Her husband was helping the horse to drag the cart up by pushing it with his shoulder. I got tea when I reached home and read German till about nine o'clock. Then Molly went away and I wrote to Coleridge. Went to bed at about twelve o'clock. I slept in Wm's bed, and I slept badly, for my thoughts were full of William.

Monday 15 February

I was starching small linen all the morning. It snowed a good deal and was terribly cold. After dinner it was fair, but I was obliged to run all the way to the foot of the White Moss to get the least bit of warmth into me. I found a letter from C.—he was much better—this was very satisfactory but his letter was not an *answer* to William's which I expected. A letter from Annette. I got tea when I reached home and then set on to reading German. I wrote part of a letter to Coleridge, went late to bed and slept badly.

Tuesday 16 February

A fine morning but I had persuaded myself not to expect William, I believe because I was afraid of being disappointed. I ironed all day. He came in just at tea time, had only seen Mary H. for a couple of hours between Emont Bridge and Hartshorn tree. Mrs C. better. He had had a difficult journey over Kirkstone, and came home by Threlkeld—his mouth and breath were very cold when he kissed me. We spent a sweet evening. He was better—had altered 'The Pedlar'. We went to bed pretty soon and we slept better than we expected and had no bad dreams. Mr Graham said he wished Wm had been with him the other day—he was riding in a post chaise and he heard a strange cry that he could not understand, the sound continued and he called to the chaise driver to stop. It was a little girl that was crying as if her heart would burst. She had got up behind the chaise and her cloak had been caught by the wheel and was jammed in and it hung there. She was crying after it. Poor thing. Mr Graham took her into the chaise and the cloak was released from the wheel but the child's misery did not cease for her cloak was torn to rags; it had been a miserable cloak before, but she had no other and it was the greatest sorrow that could befall her. Her name was Alice Fell. She had no parents, and belonged to the next town. At the next town Mr G. left money with some respectable people in the town to buy her a new cloak.

Wednesday 17 February

A miserable clashy snowy morning. We did not walk. But the old man from the hill brought us a short letter from Mary H. I copied the second part of 'Peter Bell'. William pretty well.

Thursday 18 February

A foggy morning but it cleared up in the afternoon and Wm went to Mrs Simpson's to tea. I went with him to Goan Mackereth's. Roads very dirty. I copied third part of 'Peter Bell' in his absence and began a letter to Coleridge. Wm came in with a letter from Coleridge that came by Keswick. We talked together till eleven o'clock. Then Wm got to work and was the worse for it. Hard frost.

Friday 19 February

Hard frost this morning—but it soon snowed, then thawed. A miserable afternoon. Williamson came and cut William's hair—I wrote to C. He carried the letter to Ambleside. Afterwards I wrote to Mary and Sara, tired and went early to bed.

Saturday 20 February

A very rainy morning, but it cleared up a little. We walked to Rydale. There were no letters. The roads were very dirty. We met little Dawson on horseback and desired him to bring us paper from Mrs Jameson's. After tea I wrote the first part of 'Peter Bell'. William better.

Sunday 21 February

A very wet morning. I wrote the second prologue to 'Peter Bell', then went to Mrs Olliff's. After dinner I wrote the first prologue. William walked to the tailor's while I was at Mrs O.'s it rained all the time. Snowdrops quite out, but cold and winterly—yet for all this a thrush that lives in our orchard has shouted and sung its merriest all day long. In the evening I wrote to Mrs Clarkson, and my brother Richard. Wm went to bed exhausted.

Monday 22 February

A wet morning. I lay down as soon as breakfast was over very unwell. I slept. Wm brought me four letters to bed—from Annette and Caroline, Mary and Sara, and Coleridge. C. had had another attack in his bowels—otherwise mending—M. and S. both well. M. reached Middleham the Monday night before at twelve o'clock. Tom there.—In the evening we walked to the top of the hill, then to the bridge, we hung over the wall, and looked at the deep stream below; it came with a full steady yet very rapid flow down to the lake. The sykes made a sweet sound everywhere, and looked very interesting in the twilight. That little one above Mr Olliff's house was very impressive—

Borrowdale, by John Constable

a ghostly white serpent line—it made a sound most distinctly heard of itself. The mountains were black and steep—the tops of some of them having yet snow visible, but it rained so hard last night that much of it has been washed away. After tea I was just going to write to Coleridge when Mr Simpson came in. Wm began to read 'Peter Bell' to him so I carried my writing to the kitchen fire. Wm called me upstairs to read the third part. Mr S. had brought his first engraving to let us see—he supped with us. William was tired with reading and talking and went to bed in bad spirits.

Tuesday 23 February

A misty rainy morning—the lake calm. I baked bread and pies. Before dinner worked a little at Wm's waistcoat—after dinner read German grammar. Before tea we walked into Easedale. We turned aside in the parson's field, a pretty field with three pretty prospects. Then we went to the first large field, but such a cold wind met us that we turned again. The wind seemed warm when we came out of our own door. That dear thrush was singing upon the topmost of the smooth branches of the ash tree at the top of the orchard. How long it had been perched on that same tree I cannot tell but we had heard its dear voice in the orchard the day through, along with a cheerful undersong made by our winter friends the robins. We came home by Goan's. I picked up a few mosses by the roadside, which I left at home. We then went to John's Grove. There we sat a little while looking at the fading landscape. The lake, though the objects on the shore were fading, seemed brighter than when it is a perfect day, and the island pushed itself upwards, distinct and large—all the shores marked. There was a sweet sea-like sound in the trees above our heads. We walked backwards and forwards some time for dear John's sake, then walked to look at Rydale. Darkish when we reached home and we got tea immediately with candles. William now reading in Bishop Hall—I going to read

Leathes Water, Thirlmere, by Lionel Constable

German. We have a nice singing fire, with one piece of wood. Fletcher's carts are arrived but no papers from Mrs Coleridge.

Wednesday 24 February

A rainy day. We were busy all day unripping William's coats for the tailor. William wrote to Annette, to Coleridge and the Frenchman—I received a letter from Mrs Clarkson, a very kind affecting letter which I answered telling her I would go to Eusemere when William went to Keswick—I wrote a little bit to Coleridge. We sent off these letters by Fletcher. It was a tremendous night of wind and rain. Poor Coleridge! A sad night for a traveller such as he. God be praised he was in safe quarters. Wm went out and put the letters under the door—he never felt a colder night.

Thursday 25 February

A fine mild grey beautiful morning. The tailor here. I worked at unripping. William wrote to Montagu in the morning. After dinner he went to Lloyd's—I accompanied him to the gate in the corner or turning of the vale close to the river side beyond Lenty Fleming's cottage. It was coldish and like for frost—a clear evening. I reached home just before dark, brought some mosses and ivy, then got tea, and fell to work at German. I read a good deal of Lessing's essay. William came home between nine and ten o'clock. We sat nicely together by the fire till bedtime. William not very much tired. I was bad in my bowels.

Friday 26 February

A grey morning till ten o'clock. Then the sun shone beautifully. Mrs Lloyd's children and Mrs Luff came in a chaise, were here at eleven o'clock then went to Mrs Olliff. Wm and I accompanied them to the gate. I prepared dinner, sought out 'Peter Bell', gave Wm some cold meat, and then we went to walk. We walked first to Butterlip How, where we sat and overlooked the vale, no sign of spring but the red tints of the upper twigs of the woods and single trees. Sat in the sun. Met Charles Lloyd near the bridge. Got dinner. I lay down unwell—got up to tea. Mr and Mrs Luff walked home. The Lloyds stayed till eight o'clock. We always get on better with conversation at home than elsewhere— discussion about Mrs King and Mrs Olliff.—The chaise driver brought us a letter from M. H.—a short one from C. We were perplexed about Sara's coming. I wrote to Mary. Wm closed his letter to Montagu, and wrote to Calvert and to Mrs Coleridge. Birds sang divinely today. Bowels and head bad. William better.

Saturday 27 February

We walked in the afternoon towards Rydale returning to tea. Mr Barth Simpson called after supper a little tipsy. Fletcher said he had had no papers. Wm was not very well. I sat in the orchard after dinner—we walked in the evening towards Rydale.

Sunday 28 February

Wm very ill, employed with 'The Pedlar'. We got papers in the morning. William shaved himself. I was obliged to go to bed after dinner—rose better—wrote to Sara H. and Mrs Clarkson—no walk. Disaster 'Pedlar'.

Monday 1 March

A fine pleasant day. We walked to Rydale. I went on before for the letters, brought two from M. and S. H. We climbed over the wall and read them under the shelter of a mossy rock. We met Mrs Lloyd in going—Mrs Olliff's child ill. The catkins are beautiful in the hedges. The ivy is very green. Robert Newton's paddock is greenish—that is all we see of spring. Finished and sent off the letter to Sara and wrote to Mary. Wrote again to Sara, and William wrote to Coleridge. Mrs Lloyd called when I was in bed.

Tuesday 2 March

A fine grey morning. I was baking bread and pies. After dinner I read German and a little before dinner. Wm also read. We walked on Butterlip How under the wind. It rained all the while but we had a pleasant walk. The mountains of Easedale, black or covered with snow at the tops, gave a peculiar softness to the valley. The clouds hid the tops of some of them. The valley was populous and enlivened with streams. Mrs Lloyd drove past without calling.

Wednesday 3 March

I was so unlucky as to propose to rewrite 'The Pedlar'. Wm got to work and was worn to death. We did not walk. I wrote in the afternoon.

Thursday 4 March

Before we had quite finished breakfast Calvert's man brought the horses for Wm. We had a deal to do to shave—pens to make—poems to put in order for writing, to settle the dress pack up etc. The man came before the pens were made and he was obliged to leave me with only two. Since he has left me (at half past eleven) it is now two I have been putting the drawers into order, laid by his clothes which we had thrown here and there and everywhere, filed two months' newspapers and got my dinner two boiled eggs and two apple tarts. I have set Molly on to clear the garden a little, and I myself have helped. I transplanted some snowdrops—the bees are busy—Wm has a nice bright day. It was hard frost in the night. The robins are singing sweetly. Now for my walk. I *will* be busy, I *will* look well and be well when he comes back to me. O the darling! Here is one of his bitten apples! I can hardly find in my heart to throw it into the fire. I must wash myself, then off—I walked round the two lakes crossed the stepping stones at Rydale foot. Sat down where we always sit. I was full of thoughts about my darling. Blessings on him. I came home at the foot of our own lake under Loughrigg. They are making sad ravages in the woods. Benson's wood is going and the wood above the river. The wind has blown down a fir tree on the rock that terminates John's path—I suppose the wind of Wednesday night. I read German after my return till tea time. After tea I worked and read the *Lyrical Ballads*, enchanted with 'The Idiot Boy'. Wrote to Wm then went to bed. It snowed when I went to bed.

Friday 5 March

First walked in the garden and orchard. A frosty sunny morning. After dinner I gathered mosses in Easedale. I saw before me sitting in the open field upon his sack of rags the old ragman that I know. His coat is of scarlet in a thousand patches. His breeches' knees were untied—the breeches have been given him by someone. He has a round hat pretty good, small crowned but large rimmed. When I came to him he said Is there a brigg yonder that'll carry me ow'r t'watter? He seemed half stupid. When I came home Molly had shook the carpet and cleaned everything upstairs. When I see her so happy in her work and exulting in her own importance I often think of that affecting expression which she made use of to me one evening lately. Talking of her good luck in being in this house, 'Aye Mistress them 'at's low laid would have been a proud creature could they but have seen where I is now fra what they thought mud be my doom.'—I was tired when I reached home. I sent Molly Ashburner to Rydale. No letters! I was sadly mortified. I expected one fully from Coleridge. Wrote to William. Read the *Lyrical Ballads*, got into

Ullswater, by John Glover

Grasmere Lake, by James Bourne

sad thoughts, tried at German but could not go on—read *Lyrical Ballads*.—Blessings on that brother of mine! Beautiful new moon over Silver How.

Saturday 6 March

I awoke with a bad headache and partly on that account partly for ease I lay in bed till one o'clock. At one I pulled off my nightcap—half past one sat down to breakfast. A very cold sunshiny frost. I wrote 'The Pedlar', and finished it before I went to Mr Simpson's to drink tea. Miss S. at Keswick but she came home. Mrs Jameson came in. I stayed supper. Fletcher's carts went past and I let them go with William's letter. Mr B. S. came nearly home with me. I found letters from Wm, Mary and Coleridge. I wrote to C. Sat up late and could not fall asleep when I went to bed.

Sunday 7 March

A very fine clear frost. I stitched up 'The Pedlar'—wrote out 'Ruth'—read it with the alterations. Then wrote Mary H. Read a little German—got my dinner. Mrs Lloyd called at the door; and in came William. I did not expect him till tomorrow. How glad I was. After we had talked about an hour I gave him his dinner a beefsteak, we sat talking and happy. Mr and Miss Simpson came in at tea time. William came home very well—he had been a little fatigued with reading his poems. He brought two new stanzas of 'Ruth'. We went to bed pretty soon and slept well. A mild grey evening.

Monday 8 March

A soft rain and mist. We walked to Rydale for letters. The vale looked very beautiful, in excessive simplicity yet at the same time in uncommon obscurity. The church stood alone no mountains behind. The meadows looked calm and rich bordering on the still lake; nothing else to be seen but lake and island—found a very affecting letter from

Montagu also one from Mary—we read Montagu's in walking on. Sat down to read Mary's. I came home with a bad headache and lay down. I slept but rose little better. I have got tea and am now much relieved. On Friday evening the moon hung over the northern side of the highest point of Silver How, like a gold ring snapped in two and shaven off at the ends it was so narrow. Within this ring lay the circle of the round moon, as *distinctly* to be seen as ever the enlightened moon is. William had observed the same appearance at Keswick perhaps at the very same moment hanging over the Newlands fells. Sent off a letter to Mary H. also to Coleridge and Sara, and rewrote in the evening the alterations of 'Ruth' which we sent off at the same time.

Tuesday 9 March

William was reading in Ben Jonson—he read me a beautiful poem on love. We then walked. The first part of our walk was melancholy—we went within view of Rydale then we sat in Sara's seat. We walked afterwards into Easedale. It was cold when we returned. We met Sally Newton and her water dog. We sat by the fire in the evening and read 'The Pedlar' over. William worked a little and altered it in a few places. I was not very well. Mended stockings.

Wednesday 10 March

A fine mildish morning that is, not frost. Wm read in Ben Jonson in the morning. I read a little German altered Sara's waistcoats. We then walked to Rydale—No letters! They are slashing away in Benson's wood—we walked round by the church, through Olliff's field when we returned, then home and went up into the orchard. We sat on the seat, talked a little by the fire, and then got our tea. William has since tea been talking about publishing the Yorkshire wolds poem with 'The Pedlar'.

Thursday 11 March

A fine morning. William worked at the poem of the singing bird. Just as we were sitting down to dinner we heard Mr Clarkson's voice—I ran down. William followed. He was so finely mounted that William was more intent upon the horse than the rider an offence easily forgiven for Mr Clarkson was as proud of it himself as he well could be. We ate our dinner after Mr Clarkson came. We walked with him round by the White Bridge after dinner. The vale in mist, rather the mountains, big with the rain soft and beautiful. Mr C. was sleepy and went soon to bed.

Friday 12 March

A very fine morning. We went to see Mr Clarkson off. Then we went up towards Easedale but a shower drove us back. The sun shone while it rained, and the stones of the walls and the pebbles on the road glittered like silver. When William was at Keswick I saw Jane Ashburner driving the cow along the high road from the well where she had been watering it. She had a stick in her hand and came tripping along in the jig step, as if she were dancing—her presence was bold and graceful, her cheeks flushed with health and her countenance was free and gay. William finished his poem of the singing bird. In the meantime I read the remainder of Lessing. In the evening after tea William wrote 'Alice Fell'—he went to bed tired with a wakeful mind and a weary body. A very sharp clear night.

Saturday 13 March

It was as cold as ever it has been all winter very hard frost. I baked pies bread, and seed-cake for Mr Simpson. William finished 'Alice Fell', and then he wrote the poem of the beggar woman taken from a woman whom I had seen in May—(now nearly two years ago) when John and he were at Gallow Hill. I sat with him at intervals all the morning, took down his stanzas etc. After dinner we walked to Rydale, for letters—it was terribly cold we had two or three brisk hail showers. The hail stones looked clean and pretty upon the dry clean road. Little Peggy Simpson was standing at the door catching the hail stones in her hand. She grows very like her mother. When she is sixteen years old I daresay, that to her grandmother's eye she will seem as like to what her mother was as any rose in her garden is like the rose that grew there years before. No letters at Rydale. We drank tea as soon as we reached home. After tea I read to William that account of the little boys belonging to the tall woman and an unlucky thing it was for he could not escape from those very words, and so he could not write the poem. He left it unfinished and went tired to bed. In our walk from Rydale he had got warmed with the subject and had half cast the poem.

Sunday 14 March

William had slept badly—he got up at nine o'clock, but before he rose he had finished 'The Beggar Boys'—and while we were at breakfast that is (for I had breakfasted) he, with his basin of broth before him untouched and a little plate of bread and butter he wrote the poem to a butterfly! He ate not a morsel, nor put on his stockings but sat with his shirt neck unbuttoned, and his waistcoat open while he did it. The thought first came upon him as we were talking about the pleasure we both always feel at the sight of a

Cottage in Ormathwaite, under Skiddaw, by Rev. Joseph Wilkinson

butterfly. I told him that I used to chase them a little but that I was afraid of brushing the dust off their wings, and did not catch them—he told me how they used to kill all the white ones when he went to school because they were Frenchmen. Mr Simpson came in just as he was finishing the poem. After he was gone I wrote it down and the other poems and I read them all over to him. We then called at Mr Olliff's. Mr O. walked with us to within sight of Rydale—the sun shone very pleasantly, yet it was extremely cold. We dined and then Wm went to bed. I lay upon the fur gown before the fire but I could not sleep—I lay there a long time—it is now half past five I am going to write letters. I began to write to Mrs Rawson—William rose without having slept we sat comfortably by the fire till he began to try to alter 'The Butterfly', and tired himself—he went to bed tired.

Grasmere from Red Bank, by Theophilus Aspland

Monday 15 March

We sat reading the poems and I read a little German. Mr Luff came in at one o'clock. He had a long talk with William—he went to Mr Olliff's after dinner and returned to us to tea. During his absence a sailor who was travelling from Liverpool to Whitehaven called he was faint and pale when he knocked at the door, a young man very well dressed. We sat by the kitchen fire talking with him for two hours—he told us most interesting stories of his life. His name was Isaac Chapel—he had been at sea since he was fifteen years old. He was by trade a sail-maker. His last voyage was to the coast of Guinea. He had been on board a slave ship the Captain's name Maxwell where one man had been killed a boy put to lodge with the pigs and was half eaten, one boy set to watch in the hot sun till he dropped down dead. He had been cast away in North America and had travelled thirty days among the Indians where he had been well treated—he had twice swum from a King's ship in the night and escaped, he said he would rather be in hell than be pressed. He was now going to wait in England to appear against Captain Maxwell. 'O he's a rascal, Sir, he ought to be put in the papers!' The poor man had not been in bed since Friday night. He left Liverpool at two o'clock on Saturday morning. He had called at a farmhouse to beg victuals and had been refused. The woman said she would give him nothing. 'Won't you? Then I can't help it.' He was excessively like my brother John. A letter was brought us at tea time by John Dawson from M. H. I wrote to her, to Sara about Mr Olliff's gig, and to Longman and Rees—I wrote to Mrs Clarkson by Mr Luff.

Tuesday 16 March

A very fine morning. Mrs Luff called. William went up into the orchard while she was here and wrote a part of 'The Emigrant Mother'. After dinner I read him to sleep—I read Spenser while he leaned upon my shoulder. We walked to look at Rydale. Then we walked towards Goan's. The moon was a good height above the mountains. She seemed far and distant in the sky there were two stars beside her, that twinkled in and out, and seemed almost like butterflies in motion and lightness. They looked to be far nearer to us than the moon.

Wednesday 17 March

William went up into the orchard and finished the poem. Mrs Luff and Mrs Olliff called I went with Mrs O. to the top of the White Moss—Mr O. met us and I went to their house he offered me manure for the garden. I went and sat with W. and walked backwards and forwards in the orchard till dinner time—he read me his poem. I broiled beefsteaks. After dinner we made a pillow of my shoulder, I read to him and my beloved slept—I afterwards got him the pillows and he was lying with his head on the table when Miss Simpson came in. She stayed tea. I went with her to Rydale. No letters! A sweet evening as it had been a sweet day, a grey evening, and I walked quietly along the side of Rydale lake with quiet thoughts—the hills and the lake were still—the owls had not begun to hoot, and the little birds had given over singing. I looked before me and I saw a red light upon Silver How as if coming out of the vale below,

'There was a light of most strange birth
A light that came out of the earth
And spread along the dark hill-side.'

Thus I was going on when I saw the shape of my beloved in the road at a little distance— we turned back to see the light but it was fading—almost gone. The owls hooted when we sat on the wall at the foot of White Moss. The sky broke more and more and we saw the moon now and then. John Green passed us with his cart—we sat on. When we came in sight of our own dear Grasmere, the vale looked fair and quiet in the moonshine, the church was there and all the cottages. There were high slow-travelling clouds in the sky that threw large masses of shade upon some of the mountains. We walked backwards and forwards between home and Olliff's till I was tired. William kindled and began to write the poem. We carried cloaks into the orchard and sat a while there, I left him and he nearly finished the poem. I was tired to death and went to bed before him—he came down to me and read the poem to me in bed.—A sailor begged here today going to Glasgow he spoke cheerfully in a sweet tone.

Thursday 18 March

A very fine morning. The sun shone but it was far colder than yesterday. I felt myself weak, and William charged me not to go to Mrs Lloyd's. I seemed indeed, to myself unfit for it but when he was gone I thought I would get the visit over if I could—so I ate a beefsteak thinking it would strengthen me so it did, and I went off. I had a very pleasant walk. Rydale vale was full of life and motion. The wind blew briskly and the lake was covered all over with bright silver waves that were there each the twinkling of an eye, then others rose up and took their place as fast as they went away. The rocks glittered in

the sunshine, the crows and the ravens were busy, and the thrushes and little birds sang.
I went through the fields, and sat half an hour afraid to pass a cow. The cow looked at me

and I looked at the cow and whenever I stirred the cow gave over eating. I was not very
much tired when I reached Lloyd's. I walked in the garden. Charles is all for agriculture.
Mrs L. in her kindest way. A parcel came in from Birmingham, with Lamb's play for us
and for C. They came with me as far as Rydale. As we came along Ambleside vale in the
twilight—it was a grave evening—there was something in the air that compelled me to
serious thought. The hills were large, closed in by the sky. It was nearly dark when I
parted from the Lloyds that is, night was come on and the moon was overcast. But as I
climbed Moss the moon came out from behind a mountain mass of black clouds—O the
unutterable darkness of the sky and the earth below the moon! and the glorious
brightness of the moon itself! There was a vivid sparkling streak of light at this end of
Rydale water but the rest was very dark and Loughrigg Fell and Silver How were white
and bright as if they were covered with hoar frost. The moon retired again and appeared
and disappeared several times before I reached home. Once there was no moonlight to be
seen but upon the island house and the promontory of the island where it stands, 'That
needs must be a holy place' etc. etc. I had many many exquisite feelings and when I saw
this lowly building in the waters among the dark and lofty hills, with that bright soft
light upon it, it made me more that half a poet. I was tired when I reached home. I could
not sit down to reading and tried to write verses but alas! I gave up expecting William and
went soon to bed. Fletcher's carts came home late.

Friday 19 March

A very rainy morning. I went up into the lane to collect a few green mosses to make the
chimney gay against my darling's return. Poor C.! I did not wish for, or expect him it
rained so. Mr Luff came in before my dinner. We had a long talk. He left me before four
o'clock, and about half an hour after Coleridge came in. His eyes were a little swollen

with the wind. I was much affected with the sight of him—he seemed half stupefied. William came in soon after. Coleridge went to bed late, and Wm and I sat up till four o'clock. A letter from Sara sent by Mary. They disputed about Ben Jonson. My spirits were agitated very much.

Saturday 20 March

A tolerably fine morning after eleven o'clock but when I awoke the whole vale was covered with snow. William and Coleridge walked to Borrick's. I followed but did not find them—came home and they were here—we had a little talk about going abroad. We sat pleasantly enough. After tea Wm read 'The Pedlar'. After supper we talked about various things—christening the children etc. etc. Went to bed at twelve o'clock.

Sunday 21 March

A showery day. Coleridge and William lay long in bed. We sent up to G. Mackareth's for the horse to go to Keswick but we could not have it. Went with C. to Borrick's where he left us. William was very unwell this evening. We had a sweet and tender conversation. I wrote to Mary and Sara.

Monday 22 March

A rainy day. William very poorly. Mr Luff came in after dinner and brought us two letters from Sara H. and one from poor Annette. I read Sara's letters while he was here. I finished my letters to M. and S. and wrote to my brother Richard. We talked a great deal about C. and other interesting things. We resolved to see Annette, and that Wm should go to Mary. We wrote to Coleridge not to expect us till Thursday or Friday.

Fishing by moonlight, Windermere, by Henry Bright

By John Harden

Tuesday 23 March

A mild morning. William worked at the cuckoo poem. I sewed beside him. After dinner he slept I read German, and at the closing in of day went to sit in the orchard. He came to me, and walked backwards and forwards. We talked about C. Wm repeated the poem to me. I left him there and in twenty minutes he came in, rather tired with attempting to write. He is now reading Ben Jonson I am going to read German it is about ten o'clock, a quiet night. The fire flutters and the watch ticks I hear nothing else save the breathing of my beloved and he now and then pushes his book forward and turns over a leaf. Fletcher is not come home. No letter from C.

Wednesday 24 March

We walked to Rydale for letters. It was a beautiful spring morning—warm and quiet with mists. We found a letter from M. H. I made a vow that we would not leave this country for Gallow Hill Sara and Tom not being going to the wolds. I wrote to Mary in the evening. I went to bed after dinner. William walked out and wrote Peggy Ashburner. I rose better. Wm altered 'The Butterfly' as we came from Rydale.

Thursday 25 March

We did not walk though it was a fine day. Mr Simpson drank tea with us. No letter from Coleridge.

Friday 26 March

A beautiful morning. William wrote to Annette then worked at 'The Cuckoo'. I was ill and in bad spirits—after dinner I sat two hours in the orchard. William and I walked together after tea first to the top of White Moss, then to Mr Olliff's. I left Wm and while he was absent wrote out poems. I grew alarmed and went to seek him—I met him at Mr Olliff's. He had been trying without success to alter a passage—his Silver How poem—he had written a conclusion just before he went out. While I was getting into bed he wrote 'The Rainbow'.

Saturday 27 March

A divine morning. At breakfast Wm wrote part of an ode. Mr Olliff sent the dung and Wm went to work in the garden. We sat all day in the orchard.

Sunday 28 March

We went to Keswick. Arrived wet to skin—a letter from Mary—C. was not tired with walking to meet us. I lay down after dinner with a bad headache.

Monday 29 March

A cold day. I went down to Miss Crosthwaite's to unpack the box. Wm and C. went to Ormathwaite—a letter from S. H.—bad headache and lay till after tea. Conversation with Mrs Coleridge.

Tuesday 30 March

We went to Calvert's. I was somewhat better though not well.

Part of Newlands Vale, by Rev. Joseph Wilkinson

Wednesday 31 March

Very unwell. We walked to Portinscale lay upon the turf and saw into the vale of Newlands. Up to Borrowdale and down to Keswick a soft Venetian view. I returned better. Calvert and Wilkinsons dined with us. I walked with Mrs W. to the Quakers' meeting met Wm and we walked in the field together.

Thursday 1 April

Mrs C., Wm, C. and I went to the How—a pleasant morning. We came home by Portinscale—sat for some time on the hill.

Friday 2 April

Wm and I sat all the morning in the field I nursed Derwent. Drank tea with the Miss Cockins.

Saturday 3 April

Wm went on to Skiddaw with C. We dined at Calvert's, fine day.

Sunday 4 April

We drove in the gig to Water End. I walked down to Coleridge's. Mrs C. came to Greta Bank to tea. Wm walked down with Mrs C. I repeated his verses to them. We sat pleasantly enough after supper.

Monday 5 April

We came to Eusemere. Coleridge walked with us to Threlkeld. Reached Eusemere to tea. The schoolmistress at Dacre and her scholars. Mrs C. at work in the garden. She met us.

Tuesday 6 April

Mrs C., Wm and I walked to Waterside. Wm and I walked together in the evening towards Dalemain. The moon and stars.

Windermere, Esthwaite Water and Ambleside, from Rydale Park,
by George Pickering

Wednesday 7 April

Wm's birthday. Wm went to Middleham. I walked six miles with him. It rained a little but a fine day. Broth to supper and went soon to bed.

Thursday 8 April

Mrs C. and I walked to Woodside. We slept after dinner on the sofa—sat up till half past ten. Mrs C. tired. I wrote to M. H. in the morning to Sara in the evening.

Friday 9 April

Mrs C. planting. Sent off letters. A windy morning—rough lake—sun shines very cold—a windy night. Walked in Dunmallet marked our names on a tree.

Saturday 10 April

Very cold—a stormy night, wrote to C. A letter from Wm and S. H.

Sunday 11 April

Very stormy and cold. I did not walk.

Monday 12 April

Had the mantua-maker. The ground covered with snow. Walked to T. Wilkinson's and sent for letters. The woman brought me one from Wm and Mary. It was a sharp windy night. Thomas Wilkinson came with me to Barton, and questioned me like a catechizer all the way. Every question was like the snapping of a little thread about my heart I was so full of thoughts of my half-read letter and other things. I was glad when he left me.

Cloud study, by John Constable

Then I had time to look at the moon while I was thinking over my own thoughts. The moon travelled through the clouds tinging them yellow as she passed along, with two stars near her, one larger than the other. These stars grew or diminished as they passed from or went into the clouds. At this time William as I found the next day was riding by himself between Middleham and Barnard Castle having parted from Mary. I read over my letter when I got to the house. Mr and Mrs C. were playing at cards.

Tuesday 13 April

I had slept ill and was not well and obliged to go to bed in the afternoon—Mrs C. waked me from sleep with a letter from Coleridge. After tea I went down to see the bank and walked along the lakeside to the field where Mr Smith thought of building his house. The air was become still the lake was of a bright slate colour, the hills darkening. The bays shot into the low fading shores. Sheep resting all things quiet. When I returned Jane met me—*William* was come. The surprise shot through me. He looked well but he was tired and went soon to bed after a dish of tea.

Wednesday 14 April

William did not rise till dinner time. I walked with Mrs C. I was ill out of spirits—disheartened. Wm and I took a long walk in the rain.

Thursday 15 April

It was a threatening misty morning—but mild. We set off after dinner from Eusemere. Mrs Clarkson went a short way with us but turned back. The wind was furious and we thought we must have returned. We first rested in the large boat-house, then under a furze bush opposite Mr Clarkson's. Saw the plough going in the field. The wind seized our breath the lake was rough. There was a boat by itself floating in the middle of the bay below Water Millock. We rested again in the Water Millock lane. The hawthorns are black and green, the birches here and there greenish but there is yet more of purple to be seen on the twigs. We got over into a field to avoid some cows—people working, a few primroses by the roadside, wood-sorrel flowers, the anemone, scentless violets, straw-berries, and that starry yellow flower which Mrs C. calls pile wort. When we were in the woods beyond Gowbarrow Park we saw a few daffodils close to the waterside. We fancied that the lake had floated the seeds ashore and that the little colony had so sprung up. But as we went along there were more and yet more and at last under the boughs of the trees, we saw that there was a long belt of them along the shore, about the breadth of a country turnpike road. I never saw daffodils so beautiful they grew among the mossy stones about and about them, some rested their heads upon these stones as on a pillow for weariness and the rest tossed and reeled and danced and seemed as if they verily laughed with the wind that blew upon them over the lake, they looked so gay ever glancing ever changing. This wind blew directly over the lake to them. There was here and there a little

Gowbarrow Park, Ullswater, by John Glover

knot and a few stragglers a few yards higher up but they were so few as not to disturb the simplicity and unity and life of that one busy highway. We rested again and again. The bays were stormy, and we heard the waves at different distances and in the middle of the water like the sea. Rain came on—we were wet when we reached Luff's but we called in. Luckily all was cheerless and gloomy so we faced the storm—we *must* have been wet if we had waited—put on dry clothes at Dobson's. I was very kindly treated by a young woman, the landlady looked sour but it is her way. She gave us a goodish supper. Excellent ham and potatoes. We paid seven shillings when we came away. William was sitting by a bright fire when I came downstairs. He soon made his way to the library piled up in a corner of the window. He brought out a volume of Enfield's Speaker, another miscellany, and an odd volume of Congreve's plays. We had a glass of warm rum and water. We enjoyed ourselves and wished for Mary. It rained and blew when we went to bed. N.B. Deer in Gowbarrow Park like skeletons.

Friday 16 April (Good Friday)

When I undrew my curtains in the morning, I was much affected by the beauty of the prospect and the change. The sun shone, the wind had passed away, the hills looked cheerful, the river was very bright as it flowed into the lake. The church rises up behind a little knot of rocks, the steeple not so high as an ordinary three storey house. Trees, in a row in the garden under the wall. After Wm had shaved we set forward. The valley is at first broken by little rocky woody knolls that make retiring places, fairy valleys in the vale, the river winds along under these hills travelling not in a bustle but not slowly to the lake. We saw a fisherman in the flat meadow on the other side of the water. He came towards us and threw his line over the two-arched bridge. It is a bridge of a heavy construction, almost bending inwards in the middle, but it is grey and there is a look of ancientry in the architecture of it that pleased me. As we go on the vale opens out more into one vale with somewhat of a cradle bed. Cottages with groups of trees on the side of the hills. We passed a pair of twin children two years old sat on the next bridge which we crossed a single arch. We rested again upon the turf and looked at the same bridge. We observed arches in the water occasioned by the large stones sending it down in two streams. A sheep came plunging through the river, stumbled up the bank and passed close to us, it had been frightened by an insignificant little dog on the other side, its fleece dropped a glittering shower under its belly. Primroses by the roadside, pile wort that shone like stars of gold in the sun, violets, strawberries, retired and half buried among the grass. When we came to the foot of Brothers Water I left William sitting on the bridge and went along the path on the right side of the lake through the wood. I was delighted with what I saw. The water under the boughs of the bare old trees, the simplicity of the mountains and the exquisite beauty of the path. There was one grey cottage. I repeated 'The Glowworm' as I walked along. I hung over the gate, and thought I could have stayed for ever. When I returned I found William writing a poem descriptive of the sights and sounds we saw and heard. There was the gentle flowing of the stream, the glittering lively lake, green fields without a living creature to be seen on them, behind us, a flat pasture with forty-two cattle feeding to our left the road leading to the hamlet, no smoke there, the sun shone on the bare roofs. The people were at work ploughing, harrowing and sowing—lasses spreading dung, a dog's barking now and then, cocks crowing, birds twittering, the snow in patches at the top of the highest hills, yellow palms, purple and green twigs on the birches, ashes with their glittering spikes quite

The Lake of Windermere from Ambleside, by Francis Towne

bare. The hawthorn a bright green with black stems under the oak. The moss of the oak glossy. We then went on, passed two sisters at work, *they first passed us,* one with two pitch forks in her hand. The other had a spade. We had some talk with them. They laughed aloud after we were gone perhaps half in wantonness, half boldness. William finished his poem before we got to the foot of Kirkstone. There were hundreds of cattle in the vale. There we ate our dinner. The walk up Kirkstone was very interesting. The becks among the rocks were all alive. Wm showed me the little mossy streamlet which he had before loved when he saw its bright green track in the snow. The view above Ambleside, very beautiful. There we sat and looked down on the green vale. We watched the crows at a little distance from us become white as silver as they flew in the sunshine, and when they went still further they looked like shapes of water passing over the green fields. The whitening of Ambleside church is a great deduction from the beauty of it seen from this point. We called at the Luffs', the Boddingtons there did not go in and went round by the fields. I pulled off my stockings intending to wade the beck but I was obliged to put them on and we climbed over the wall at the bridge. The post passed us. No letters! Rydale lake was in its own evening brightness, the islands and points distinct. Jane Ashburner came up to us when we were sitting upon the wall. We rode in her cart to Tom Dawson's. All well. The garden looked pretty in the half moonlight–half daylight. As we went up the vale of Brothers Water more and more cattle feeding a hundred of them.

Saturday 17 April

A mild warm rain. We sat in the garden all the morning. William dug a little. I

Grasmere Lake and Village, by George Pickering

transplanted a honeysuckle. The lake was still the sheep on the island reflected in the water, like the grey deer we saw in Gowbarrow Park. We walked after tea by moonlight. I had been in bed in the afternoon and William had slept in his chair. We walked towards Rydale first then backwards and forwards below Mr Olliff's. The village was beautiful in the moonlight. Helm Crag we observed very distinct. The dead hedge round Benson's field bound together at the top by an interlacing of ash sticks which made a chain of silver when we faced the moon. A letter from C., and also from S. H. I saw a robin chasing a scarlet butterfly this morning.

Sunday 18 April

I lay in bed late. Again a mild grey morning with rising vapours. We sat in the orchard. William wrote the poem on the robin and the butterfly. I went to drink tea at Luff's but as we did not dine till six o'clock it was late. It was mist and small rain all the way but very pleasant. William met me at Rydale—Aggie accompanied me thither. We sat up late. He met me with the conclusion of the poem of the robin. I read it to him in bed. We left out some lines.

Monday 19 April

A mild rain very warm. Wm worked in the garden. I made pies and bread. After dinner the mist cleared away and sun shone. William walked to Luff's. I was not very well and went to bed. Wm came home pale and tired. I could not rest when I got to bed.

Tuesday 20 April

A beautiful morning. The sun shone. William wrote a conclusion to the poem of the butterfly—'I've watched you now a full half-hour'. I was quite out of spirits and went into the orchard. When I came in he had finished the poem. We sat in the orchard after dinner, it was a beautiful afternoon. The sun shone upon the level fields and they grew greener beneath the eye—houses village all cheerful—people at work. We sat in the orchard and repeated 'The Glowworm' and other poems. Just when William came to a well or a trough which there is in Lord Darlington's park he began to write that poem of the glowworm. Not being able to write upon the long trot. Interrupted in going through the town of Staindrop. Finished it about two miles and a half beyond Staindrop. He did not feel the jogging of the horse while he was writing but when he had done he felt the effect of it and his fingers were cold with his gloves. His horse fell with him on the other side of St Helen's, Auckland.—So much for the glowworm. It was written coming from Middleham on Monday April 12th 1802. On Tuesday 20th when we were sitting after tea Coleridge came to the door. I startled Wm with my voice. C. came up palish but I afterwards found he looked well. William was not well and I was in low spirits.

Wednesday 21 April

William and I sauntered a little in the garden. Coleridge came to us and repeated the verses he wrote to Sara. I was affected with them and was on the whole, not being well, in miserable spirits. The sunshine—the green fields and the fair sky made me sadder; even the little happy sporting lambs seemed but sorrowful to me. The pile wort spread out on the grass a thousand shining stars. The primroses were there and the remains of a few daffodils. The well which we cleaned out last night is still but a little muddy pond, though full of water. I went to bed after dinner, could not sleep, went to bed again. Read Ferguson's life and a poem or two—fell asleep for five minutes and awoke better. We got tea. Sat comfortably in the evening. I went to bed early.

Thursday 22 April

A fine mild morning. We walked into Easedale. The sun shone. Coleridge talked of his plan of sowing the laburnum in the woods. The waters were high for there had been a great quantity of rain in the night. I was tired and sat under the shade of a holly tree that grows upon a rock. I sat there and looked down the stream. I then went to the single holly behind that single rock in the field and sat upon the grass till they came from the waterfall. I saw them there and heard Wm flinging stones into the river whose roaring was loud even where I was. When they returned William was repeating the poem 'I have thoughts that are fed by the sun'. It had been called to his mind by the dying away of the stunning of the waterfall when he came behind a stone. When we had got into the vale a heavy rain came on. We saw a family of little children sheltering themselves under a wall before the rain came on. They sat in a row making a canopy for each other of their clothes. The servant lass was planting potatoes near them. Coleridge changed his clothes. We were all wet. Wilkinson came in while we were at dinner. Coleridge and I after dinner drank blackcurrants and water.

Friday 23 April

It being a beautiful morning we set off at eleven o'clock intending to stay out of doors all the morning. We went towards Rydale and before we got to Tom Dawson's we determined to go under Nab Scar. Thither we went. The sun shone and we were lazy. Coleridge pitched upon several places to sit down upon but we could not be all of one mind respecting sun and shade so we pushed on to the foot of the Scar. It was very grand when we looked up very stony, here and there a budding tree. William observed that the umbrella yew tree that breasts the wind had lost its character as a tree and had become something like to solid wood. Coleridge and I pushed on before. We left William sitting on the stones feasting with silence—and C. and I sat down upon a rocky seat—a couch it might be under the bower of William's eglantine, Andrew's broom. He was below us and we could see him. He came to us and repeated his poems while we sat beside him upon the ground. He had made himself a seat in the crumbly ground. After we had lingered long looking into the vales—Ambleside vale with the copses the village under the hill and the green fields—Rydale with a lake all alive and glittering yet but little stirred by breezes, and our own dear Grasmere first making a little round lake of nature's own with never a house never a green field but the copses and the bare hills enclosing it and the river flowing out of it. Above rose the Coniston Fells in their own shape and colour. Not man's hills but all for themselves the sky and the clouds and a few wild creatures. C. went to search for something new. We saw him climbing up towards a rock. He called us and we found him in a bower, the sweetest that was ever seen. The rock on one side is very high and all covered with ivy which hung loosely about and bore bunches of brown berries. On the other side it was higher than my head. We looked down upon the Ambleside vale that seemed to wind away from us the village *lying* under the hill. The fir tree island was reflected beautifully. We now first saw that the trees are planted in rows. About this bower there is mountain ash, common ash, yew tree, ivy, holly, hawthorn mosses and flowers, and a carpet of moss. Above at the top of the rock there is another spot—it is scarce a bower, a little parlour only not *enclosed* by walls but shaped out for a resting place by the rocks and the ground rising about it. It had a sweet moss carpet. We resolved to go and plant flowers in both these places tomorrow. We wished for Mary and Sara. Dined late. After dinner Wm and I worked in the garden. C. read. A letter from Sara.

Saturday 24 April

A very wet day. William called me out to see a waterfall behind the barberry tree—We walked in the evening to Rydale. Coleridge and I lingered behind. C. stopped up the little runner by the roadside to make a lake. We all stood to look at Glowworm Rock—a primrose that grew there, and just looked out on the road from its own sheltered bower. The clouds moved as William observed in one regular body like a multitude in motion a sky all clouds over, not one cloud. On our return it broke a little out and we saw here and there a star. One appeared but for a moment in a lake of pale blue sky.

Sunday 25 April

After breakfast we set off with Coleridge towards Keswick. Wilkinson overtook us near the potter's and interrupted our discourse. C. got into a gig with Mr Beck, and drove away from us. A shower came on but it was soon over. We spent the morning in the orchard. Read the 'Prothalamium' of Spenser—walked backwards and forwards. Mr

In Yewdale, near Coniston, by John Harper

Simpson drank tea with us. I was not well before tea. Mr S. sent us some quills by Molly Ashburner and his brother's book. The Luffs called at the door.

Monday 26 April

I copied Wm's poems for Coleridge. Letters from Peggy and Mary H.—wrote to Peggy and Coleridge. A terrible rain and wind all day. Went to bed at twelve o'clock.

Tuesday 27 April

A fine morning. Mrs Luff called. I walked with her to the boat-house. William met me at the top of the hill with his fishing-rod in his hand. I turned with him and we sat on the hill looking to Rydale. I left him intending to join him but he came home, and said his lines would not stand the pulling. He had had several bites. He sat in the orchard—I made bread. Miss Simpson called. I walked with her to Goan's. When I came back I found that he and John Fisher had cleaned out the well. John had sodded about the bee-stand. In the evening he began to write 'The Tinker'. We had a letter and verses from Coleridge.

Wednesday 28 April

A fine sunny but coldish morning. I copied 'The Prioress's Tale'. Wm was in the orchard. I went to him—he worked away at his poem—though he was ill and tired. I happened to say that when I was a child I would not have pulled a strawberry blossom. I left him and wrote out 'The Manciple's Tale'. At dinner time he came in with the poem of 'Children Gathering Flowers'—but it was not quite finished and it kept him long off his dinner. It is now done he is working at 'The Tinker'. He promised me he would get his tea and do no more but I have got mine an hour and a quarter and he has scarcely begun his. I am not quite well. We have let the bright sun go down without walking. Now a heavy shower comes on and I guess we shall not walk at all. I wrote a few lines to Coleridge. Then we walked backwards and forwards between our house and Olliff's. We talked about T. Hutchinson and Bell Addison. William left me sitting on a stone. When we came in we corrected the Chaucers but I could not finish them tonight. Went to bed.

Thursday 29 April

A beautiful morning. The sun shone and all was pleasant. We sent off our parcel to Coleridge by the waggon. Mr Simpson heard the cuckoo today. Before we went out after I had written down 'The Tinker' (which William finished this morning) Luff called. He was very lame, limped into the kitchen—he came on a little pony. We then went to John's Grove, sat a while at first. Afterwards William lay, and I lay in the trench under the fence—he with his eyes shut and listening to the waterfalls and the birds. There was no one waterfall above another—it was a sound of waters in the air—the voice of the air. William heard me breathing and rustling now and then but we both lay still, and unseen by one another. He thought that it would be as sweet thus to lie so in the grave, to hear the *peaceful* sounds of the earth and just to know that our dear friends were near. The lake was still. There was a boat out. Silver How reflected with delicate purple and yellowish hues as I have seen Spar. Lambs on the island and running races together by the half dozen in the round field near us. The copses green*ish*, hawthorn green.—Came home to dinner then went to Mr Simpson. We rested a long time under a wall. Sheep and lambs were in the field—cottages smoking. As I lay down on the grass, I observed the

Grasmere, by William Havell

glittering silver line on the ridges of the backs of the sheep, owing to their situation respecting the sun—which made them look beautiful but with something of strangeness, like animals of another kind—as if belonging to a more splendid world. Met old Mr S. at the door—Mrs S. poorly. I got mullens and pansies. I was sick and ill and obliged to come home soon. We went to bed immediately—I slept upstairs. The air coldish where it was felt somewhat frosty.

Friday 30 April

We came into the orchard directly after breakfast, and sat there. The lake was calm—the sky cloudy. We saw two fishermen by the lakeside. William began to write the poem of the celandine. I wrote to Mary H. sitting on the fur gown. Walked backwards and forwards with William—he repeated his poem to me. Then he got to work again and could not give over—he had not finished his dinner till five o'clock. After dinner we took up the fur gown into The Hollins above. We found a sweet seat and thither we will often go. We spread the gown put on each a cloak and there we lay. William fell asleep—he had a bad headache owing to his having been disturbed the night before with reading C.'s letter which Fletcher had brought to the door. I did not sleep but I lay with half shut eyes looking at the prospect as in a vision almost I was so resigned to it. Loughrigg Fell was the most distant hill, then came the lake slipping in between the copses and above the copse the round swelling field, nearer to me a wild intermixture of rocks trees, and slacks of grassy ground.—When we turned the corner of our little shelter we saw the church and the whole vale. It is a blessed place. The birds were about us on all sides—skobbys robins bullfinches. Crows now and then flew over our heads as we were warned by the sound of the beating of the air above. We stayed till the light of day was going and the little birds had begun to settle their singing. But there was a thrush not far off that seemed to sing louder and clearer than the thrushes had sung when it was quite day. We came in at eight o'clock, got tea. Wrote to Coleridge, and I wrote to Mrs Clarkson part of a letter. We went to bed at twenty minutes past eleven with prayers that Wm might sleep well.

Saturday 1 May

Rose not till half past eight. A heavenly morning. As soon as breakfast was over we went into the garden and sowed the scarlet beans about the house. It was a clear sky a heavenly morning. I sowed the flowers William helped me. We then went and sat in the orchard till dinner time. It was very hot. William wrote 'The Celandine'. We planned a shed for the sun was too much for us. After dinner we went again to our old resting place in The Hollins under the rock. We first lay under a holly where we saw nothing but the holly tree and a budding elm and the sky above our heads. But that holly tree had a beauty about it more than its own, knowing as we did where we were. When the sun had got low enough we went to the rock shade. Oh the overwhelming beauty of the vale below—greener than green. Two ravens flew high high in the sky and the sun shone upon their bellies and their wings long after there was none of his light to be seen but a little space on the top of Loughrigg Fell. We went down to tea at eight o'clock—had lost the poem and returned after tea. The landscape was fading, sheep and lambs quiet among the rocks. We walked towards King's and backwards and forwards. The sky was perfectly cloudless. N.B. Is it often so? Three solitary stars in the middle of the blue vault one or two on the points of the high hills. Wm wrote 'The Celandine' second part tonight. Heard the cuckoo today this first of May.

Sunday 2 May

Again a heavenly morning. Letter from Coleridge.

Tuesday 4 May

William had slept pretty well and though he went to bed nervous and jaded in the extreme he rose refreshed. I wrote 'The Leech Gatherer' for him which he had begun the night before and of which he wrote several stanzas in bed this Monday morning. It was very hot, we called at Mr Simpson's door as we passed but did not go in. We rested several times by the way, read and repeated 'The Leech Gatherer'. We were almost melted before we were at the top of the hill. We saw Coleridge on the Wytheburn side of the water. He crossed the beck to us. Mr Simpson was fishing there. William and I ate a luncheon, then went on towards the waterfall. It is a glorious wild solitude under that lofty purple crag. It stood upright by itself. Its own self and its shadow below, one mass— all else was sunshine. We went on further. A bird at the top of the crags was flying round and round and looked in thinness and transparency, shape and motion like a moth. We climbed the hill but looked in vain for a shade except at the foot of the great waterfall, and there we did not like to stay on account of the loose stones above our heads. We came down and rested upon a moss covered rock, rising out of the bed of the river. There we lay ate our dinner and stayed there till about four o'clock or later. Wm and C. repeated and read verses. I drank a little brandy and water and was in Heaven. The stags horn is very beautiful and fresh springing upon the fells. Mountain ashes, green. We drank tea at a farmhouse. The woman had not a pleasant countenance, but was civil enough. She had a pretty boy a year old whom she suckled. We parted from Coleridge at Sara's Crag after having looked at the letters which C. carved in the morning. I kissed them all. Wm deepened the T with C.'s penknife. We sat afterwards on the wall, seeing the sun go down and the reflections in the still water. C. looked well and parted from us cheerfully, hopping up upon the side stones. On the Rays we met a woman with two little girls one in her arms the other about four years old walking by her side, a pretty little thing, but half starved. She had on a pair of slippers that had belonged to some gentleman's child, down at the heels—it was not easy to keep them on but, poor thing! young as she was, she walked carefully with them. Alas too young for such cares and such travels. The mother when we accosted her told us that her husband had left her and gone off with another woman and how she 'pursued' them. Then her fury kindled and her eyes rolled about. She changed again to tears. She was a Cockermouth woman thirty years of age—a child at Cockermouth when I was. I was moved and gave her a shilling—I believe sixpence more than I ought to have given. We had the crescent moon with the 'auld moon in her arms'. We rested often always upon the bridges. Reached home at about ten o'clock. The Lloyds had been here in our absence. We went soon to bed. I repeated verses to William while he was in bed—he was soothed and I left him. 'This is the spot' over and over again.

Wednesday 5 May

A very fine morning rather cooler than yesterday. We planted three fourths of the bower. I made bread. We sat in the orchard. The thrush sang all day as he always sings. I wrote to the Hutchinsons and to Coleridge—packed off *Thalaba*. William had kept off work till near bed time when we returned from our walk—then he began again and went to bed very nervous. We walked in the twilight and walked till night came on. The moon

17

The Leech-gatherer

There was a roaring in the wind all night
The rain came heavily and fell in floods
But now the sun is rising calm and bright
The Birds are singing in the distant woods
Over his own sweet voice the Stock-dove broods
The Jay makes answer as the magpie chatters
And all the air is fill'd with pleasant noise of
                                                              waters

All things that love the sun are out of doors
The sky rejoices in the morning's birth
The grass is bright with rain drops: on the moor
The Hare is running races in her mirth
And with her feet she from the plashy earth
Raises a mist which glittering in the sun
Runs with her all the way wherever she doth run.

I was a Traveller upon the moor
I saw the hare that raced about with joy
I heard the woods and distant waters roar
Or heard them not, as happy as a Boy
The pleasant season did my heart employ
My old remembrances went from me wholly
And all the ways of men so vain & melancholy

But as it sometimes chanceth from the might
Of joy in minds that can no farther go
As high as we have mounted in delight
In our dejection do we sink as low
To me that morning did it happen so
And fears and fancies thick upon me came
Dim sadness & blind thoughts I knew not nor could
                                                              name.

A page of 'The Leech Gatherer'

Lodore Falls, by Francis Towne

had the old moon in her arms but not so plain to be seen as the night before. When we went to bed it was a boat without the circle. I read 'The Lover's Complaint' to Wm in bed and left him composed.

Thursday 6 May

A sweet morning. We have put the finishing stroke to our bower and here we are sitting in the orchard. It is one o'clock. We are sitting upon a seat under the wall which I found my brother building up when I came to him with his apple—he had intended that it should have been done before I came. It is a nice cool shady spot. The small birds are singing, lambs bleating, cuckoo calling. The thrush sings by fits. Thomas Ashburner's axe is going quietly (without passion) in the orchard. Hens are cackling, flies humming, the women talking together at their doors: plum and pear trees are in blossom—apple trees greenish the opposite woods green, the crows are cawing. We have heard ravens. The ash trees are in blossom, birds flying all about us. The stitchwort is coming out, there is one budding Lychnis, the primroses are passing their prime. Celandine violets and wood sorrel for ever more little geraniums and pansies on the wall. We walked in the evening to Tail End to enquire about hurdles for the orchard shed and about Mr Luff's flower. The flower dead—no hurdles. I went to look at the falling wood—Wm also when he had been at Benson's went with me. They have left a good many small oak trees but we dare not hope that they are all to remain. The ladies are come to Mr Gell's cottage. We saw them as we went and their light when we returned. When we came in we found a magazine and review and a letter from Coleridge with verses to Hartley and Sara H. We read the review, etc. The moon was a perfect boat a silver boat when we were out in the evening. The birch tree is all over green in *small* leaf more light and elegant than when it is full out. It bent to the breezes as if for the love of its own delightful motions. Sloe thorns and hawthorns in the hedges.

Friday 7 May

William had slept uncommonly well so, feeling himself strong, he fell to work at 'The Leech Gatherer'. He wrote hard at it till dinner time, then he gave over tired to death—he had finished the poem. I was making Derwent's frocks. After dinner we sat in the orchard. It was a thick hazy dull air. The thrush sang almost continually—the little birds were more than usually busy with their voices. The sparrows are now full fledged. The nest is so full that they lie upon one another, they sit quietly in their nest with closed mouths. I walked to Rydale after tea which we drank by the kitchen fire. The evening very dull—a terrible kind of threatening brightness at sunset above Easedale. The sloe thorn beautiful in the hedges, and in the wild spots higher up among the hawthorns. No letters. William met me. He had been digging in my absence and cleaning the well. We walked up beyond Lewthwaite's—a very dull sky, coolish crescent moon now and then. I had a letter brought me from Mrs Clarkson. While we were walking in the orchard I observed the sorrel leaves opening at about nine o'clock. William went to bed tired with thinking about a poem.

Saturday 8 May

We sowed the scarlet beans in the orchard, I read *Henry V* there. William lay on his back on the seat. I wept, for names, sounds faiths delights and duties lost—taken from a poem upon Cowley's wish to retire to the plantations. Read in the review. After dinner William added a step to the orchard steps.

Sunday 9 May

The air considerably colder today but the sun shone all day. William worked at 'The Leech Gatherer' almost incessantly from morning till tea time. I copied 'The Leech Gatherer' and other poems for Coleridge. I was oppressed and sick at heart for he wearied himself to death. After tea he wrote two stanzas in the manner of Thomson's 'Castle of Indolence', and was tired out. Bad news of Coleridge.

Monday 10 May

A fine clear morning but coldish. William is still at work though it is past ten o'clock—he will be tired out I am sure. My heart fails in me. He worked a little at odd things, but after dinner he gave over. An affecting letter from Mary H. We sat in the orchard before dinner. Old Joyce spent the day. I wrote to Mary H. Mrs Jameson and Miss Simpson called just when William was going to bed at eight o'clock. I wrote to Coleridge sent off reviews and poems, went to bed at twelve o'clock. William did not sleep till three o'clock.

Tuesday 11 May

A cool air. William finished the stanzas about C. and himself—he did not go out today. Miss Simpson came into tea which was lucky enough for it interrupted his labours. I walked with her to Rydale—the evening cool—the moon only now and then to be seen—the lake purple as we went—primroses still in abundance. William did not meet me. He completely finished his poems I finished Derwent's frocks. We went to bed at twelve o'clock. Wm pretty well—he looked very well. He complains that he gets cold in his chest.

Wednesday 12 May

A sunshiny but coldish morning. We walked into Easedale and returned by George Rownson's and the lane. We brought home heckberry blossom, crab blossom—the anemone nemorosa—marsh marigold—speedwell, that beautiful blue one the colour of the blue-stone or glass used in jewellery, with its beautiful pearl-like chives. Anemones are in abundance and still the dear dear primroses violets in beds, pansies in abundance and the little celandine. I pulled a branch of the taller celandine. Butterflies of all colours—I often see some small ones of a pale purple lilac or Emperor's eye colour something of the colour of that large geranium which grows by the lakeside. Wm observed the beauty of Geordy Green's house. We see it from our orchard. Wm pulled ivy with beautiful berries—I put it over the chimney-piece. Sat in the orchard the hour before dinner—coldish. We have now dined. My head aches—William is sleeping in the window. In the evening we were sitting at the table, writing, when we were roused by Coleridge's voice below—he had walked, looked palish but was not much tired. We sat up till one o'clock all together then William went to bed and I sat with C. in the sitting room (where he slept) till a quarter past two o'clock. Wrote to M. H.

Thursday 13 May

The day was very cold, with snow showers. Coleridge had intended going in the morning

Storm on Keswick Lake, by John Downman

to Keswick but the cold and showers hindered him. We went with him after tea as far as the plantations by the roadside descending to Wytheburn—he did not look very well when we parted from him.—We sat an hour at Mr Simpson's.

Friday 14 May

A very cold morning—hail and snow showers all day. We went to Brothers' wood, intending to get plants and to go along the shore of the lake to the foot. We did go a part of the way, but there was no pleasure in stepping along that difficult sauntering road in this ungenial weather. We turned again and walked backwards and forwards in Brothers' wood. William teased himself with seeking an epithet for the cuckoo. I sat a while upon my last summer's seat the mossy stone—William's unemployed beside me, and the space between where Coleridge has so often lain. The oak trees are just putting forth yellow knots of leaves. The ashes with their flowers passing away and leaves coming out. The blue hyacinth is not quite full blown—gowans are coming out—marsh marigolds in full glory—the little star plant a star without a flower. We took home a great load of gowans and planted them in the cold about the orchard. After dinner I worked bread then came and mended stockings beside William. He fell asleep. After tea I walked to Rydale for letters. It was a strange night. The hills were covered over with a slight covering of hail or snow, just so as to give them a hoary winter look with the black rocks. The woods looked miserable, the coppices green as grass which looked quite unnatural and they seemed half shrivelled up as if they shrunk from the air. O thought I! what a beautiful

gowans: daisies

Cottage in the vale of Embleton, by Rev. Joseph Wilkinson

thing God has made winter to be by stripping the trees and letting us see their shapes and forms. What a freedom does it seem to give to the storms! There were several new flowers out but I had no pleasure in looking at them. I walked as fast as I could back again with my letter from S. H. which I skimmed over at Tommy Fleming's. Met Wm at the top of White Moss. We walked a little beyond Olliff's. Near ten when we came in. Wm and Molly had dug the ground and planted potatoes in my absence. We wrote to Coleridge—sent off a letter to Annette, bread and frocks to the C.'s—Went to bed at half past eleven. William very nervous—after he was in bed haunted with altering 'The Rainbow'.

Saturday 15 May

It is now a quarter past ten and he is not up. Miss Simpson called when I was in bed. I have been in the garden. It looks fresh and neat in spite of the frost. Molly tells me they had thick ice on a jug at their door last night.

A very cold and cheerless morning. I sat mending stockings all the morning. I read in Shakespeare. William lay very late because he slept ill last night. It snowed this morning just like Christmas. We had a melancholy letter from Coleridge just at bed time. It distressed me very much and I resolved upon going to Keswick the next day.

Sunday 16 May

William was at work all the morning. I did not go to Keswick. A sunny cold frosty day. A snow shower at night. We were a good while in the orchard in the morning.

Monday 17 May

William was not well—he went with me to Wytheburn water. He left me in a post chaise. Hail showers snow and cold attacked me. The people were graving peats under Nadel Fell.—A lark and thrush singing near Coleridge's house. Bancrofts there. A letter from M. H.

Tuesday 18 May

Terribly cold. Coleridge not well. Froude called, Wilkinsons called, I not well. C. and I walked in the evening in the garden. Warmer in the evening. Wrote to M. and S.

Wednesday 19 May

A grey morning—not quite so cold. C. and I set off at half past nine o'clock. Met William, near the six mile stone. We sat down by the roadside, and then went to Wytheburn water. Longed to be at the island. Sat in the sun, Coleridge's bowels bad, mine also. We drank tea at John Stanley's—the evening cold and clear. A glorious light on Skiddaw. I was tired—brought a cloak down from Mr Simpson's. Packed up books for Coleridge then got supper and went to bed.

Thursday 20 May

A frosty clear morning. I lay in bed late. William got to work. I was somewhat tired. We sat in the orchard sheltered all the morning. In the evening there was a fine rain. We received a letter from Coleridge, telling us that he wished us not to go to Keswick.

Friday 21 May

A very warm gentle morning—a little rain. Wm wrote two sonnets on Buonaparte after I had read Milton's sonnets to him. In the evening he went with Mr Simpson with Borrick's boat to gather ling in Bainriggs. I planted about the well—was much heated and I think I caught cold.

Windermere, by John Harden

Saturday 22 May

A very hot morning. A hot wind as if coming from a sand desert. We met Coleridge, he was sitting under Sara's Rock when we reached him. He turned with us. We sat a long time under the wall of a sheep-fold. Had some interesting melancholy talk about his private affairs. We drank tea at a farmhouse. The woman was very kind. There was a woman with three children travelling from Workington to Manchester. The woman served them liberally. Afterwards she said that she never suffered any to go away without a trifle 'sec as we have'. The woman at whose house we drank tea the last time was rich and senseless—she said 'she never served any but their own poor'.—C. came home with us. We sat some time in the orchard. Then they came in to supper—mutton chops and potatoes. Letters from S. and M. H.

Sunday 23 May

I sat with C. in the orchard all the morning. I was ill in the afternoon, took laudanum. We walked in Bainriggs after tea. Saw the juniper—umbrella shaped.—C. went to Sara and Mary Points, joined us on White Moss.

Monday 24 May

A very hot morning. We were ready to go off with Coleridge, but foolishly sauntered and Miss Taylor and Miss Stanley called. William and Coleridge and I went afterwards to the top of the Rays. I was ill and left them, lay down at Mrs Simpson's. I had sent off a letter to Mary by C. I wrote again and to C., then went to bed. William slept not till five o'clock.

Tuesday 25 May

Very hot—I went to bed after dinner.—We walked in the evening. Papers and short note from C.—again no sleep for Wm.

Wednesday 26 May

I was very unwell—went to bed again after dinner. We walked a long time backwards and forwards between John's Grove and the lane upon the turf. A beautiful night, not cloudless. It has never been so since May day.

Thursday 27 May

I was in bed all day—very ill. William wrote to Richard Christopher and Cook. Wm went after tea into the orchard. I slept in his bed—he slept downstairs.

Friday 28 May

I was much better than yesterday, though poorly. William tired himself with hammering at a passage. After dinner he was better and I grew better. We sat in the orchard. The sky cloudy the air sweet and cool. The young bullfinches in their party coloured raiment bustle about among the blossoms and poise themselves like wire-dancers or tumblers, shaking the twigs and dashing off the blossoms. There is yet one primrose in the orchard. The stitchwort is fading. The wild columbines are coming into beauty. The vetches are in

Borrowdale, by Joseph Powell

abundance, blossoming and seeding. That pretty little waxy-looking dial-like yellow flower, the speedwell, and some others whose names I do not yet know. The wild columbines are coming into beauty—some of the gowans fading. In the garden we have lilies and many other flowers. The scarlet beans are up in crowds. It is now between eight and nine o'clock. It has rained sweetly for two hours and a half—the air is very mild. The heckberry blossoms are dropping off fast, almost gone—barberries are in beauty—snowballs coming forward—May roses blossoming.

Saturday 29 May

I was much better. I made bread and a wee rhubarb tart and batter pudding for William. We sat in the orchard after dinner. William finished his poem on going for Mary. I wrote it out. I wrote to Mary H., having received a letter from her in the evening. A sweet day. We nailed up the honeysuckles, and hoed the scarlet beans.

The shore of Keswick Lake, by R. R. Reinagle

Sunday 30 May

I wrote to Mrs Clarkson. It was a clear but cold day. The Simpsons called in the evening. I had been obliged to go to bed before tea and was unwell all day. Gooseberries a present from Peggy Hodgson. I wrote to my aunt Cookson.

Monday 31 May

I was much better. We sat out all the day. Mary Jameson dined. I wrote out the poem on 'Our Departure' which he seemed to have finished. In the evening Miss Simpson brought us a letter from M. H. and a complimentary and critical letter to W. from John Wilson of Glasgow post paid. I went a little way with Miss S. My tooth broke today. They will soon be gone. Let that pass I shall be beloved—I want no more.

Tuesday 1 June

A very sweet day, but a sad want of rain. We went into the orchard before dinner after I had written to M. H. Then on to Mr Olliff's intakes. We found some torn birds' nests. The columbine was growing upon the rocks, here and there a solitary plant—sheltered and shaded by the tufts and bowers of trees. It is a graceful slender creature, a female seeking retirement and growing freest and most graceful where it is most alone. I observed that the more shaded plants were always the tallest. A short note and gooseberries from Coleridge.

Wednesday 2 June

In the morning we observed that the scarlet beans were drooping in the leaves in great numbers owing, we guess, to an insect. We sat a while in the orchard—then we went to the old carpenter's about the hurdles. Yesterday an old man called, a grey-headed man, above seventy years of age. He said he had been a soldier, that his wife and children had died in Jamaica. He had a beggar's wallet over his shoulders, a coat of shreds and patches altogether of a drab colour—he was tall and though his body was bent he had the look of one used to have been upright. I talked a while to him, and then gave him a piece of cold bacon and a penny. Said he 'You're a fine woman!' I could not help smiling. I suppose he meant 'You're a kind woman.' Afterwards a woman called travelling to Glasgow. After dinner William was very unwell. We went into Frank's field, crawled up the little glen and planned a seat then went to Mr Olliff's Hollins and sat there—found a beautiful shell-like purple fungus in Frank's field. After tea we walked to Butterlip How and backwards and forwards there. All the young oak tree leaves are dry as powder. A cold south wind portending rain. After we came in we sat in deep silence at the window—I on a chair and William with his hand on my shoulder. We were deep in silence and love, a blessed hour. We drew to the fire before bed time and ate some broth for our suppers. I ought to have said that on Tuesday evening, namely June 1st, we walked upon the turf near John's Grove. It was a lovely night. The clouds of the western sky reflected a saffron light upon the upper end of the lake. All was still. We went to look at Rydale. There was an alpine fire-like red upon the tops of the mountains. This was gone when we came in view of the lake. But we saw the lake in a new and most beautiful point of view between two little rocks, and behind a small ridge that had concealed it from us.—This White Moss a place made for all kinds of beautiful works of art and nature, woods and valleys, fairy valleys and fairy tarns, miniature mountains, alps above alps. Little John Dawson came past us from the woods with a huge stick over his shoulder.

Thursday 3 June

A very fine rain. I lay in bed till ten o'clock. William much better than yesterday. We walked into Easedale—sheltered in a cow-house. Came home wet. The cuckoo sang and we watched the little birds as we sat at the door of the cow-house. The oak copses are brown, as in autumn with the late frosts—scattered over with green trees, birches or hazels. The ashes are coming into full leaf—some of them injured. We came home quite wet. We have been reading the life and some of the writings of poor Logan since dinner. 'And everlasting longings for the lost.' It is an affecting line. There are many affecting lines and passages in his poems. William is now sleeping, with the window open lying on the window seat. The thrush is singing. There are I do believe a thousand buds on the honeysuckle tree all small and far from blowing, save one that is retired behind the twigs close to the wall and as snug as a bird's nest. John's rose tree is very beautiful blended with the honeysuckle.

On Tuesday evening when we were among the rocks we saw in the woods what seemed to be a man, resting or looking about him—he had a piece of wood near him. William was on before me when we returned, and as I was going up to him, I found that this supposed man was John Dawson. I spoke to him and I suppose he thought I asked him what my brother had said to him before, for he replied: '*William* asks me how my head is.' Poor fellow!—he says it is worse and worse and he talks as if he were afraid of putting his body in motion.

Yesterday morning William walked as far as The Swan with Aggy Fisher. She was going to attend upon Goan's dying infant. She said, 'There are many heavier crosses than the death of an infant', and went on, 'There was a woman in this vale who buried four grown-up children in one year, and I have heard her say when many years were gone by that she had more pleasure in thinking of those four than of her living children, for as children get up and have families of their own their duty to their parents "*wears out and weakens*". She could trip lightly by the graves of those who died when they were young, with a light step, as she went to church on a Sunday.'

We walked while dinner was getting ready up into Mr King's Hollins. I was weak and made my way down alone, for Wm took a difficult way. After dinner we walked upon the turf path—a showery afternoon. A very affecting letter came from M. H. while I was sitting in the window reading Milton's 'Penseroso' to William. I answered this letter before I went to bed.

Friday 4 June

It was a very sweet morning. There had been much rain in the night. William had slept miserably but knowing this I lay in bed while he got some sleep but was much disordered, he shaved himself then we went into the orchard. Dined late. In the evening we walked on our favourite path. Then we came in and sat in the orchard. The evening was dark and warm—a tranquil night. I left William in the orchard. I read *Mother Hubberd's Tale* before I went to bed.

Saturday 5 June

A fine showery morning. I made both pies and bread, but we first walked into Easedale, and sat under the oak trees upon the mossy stones. There were one or two slight showers. The gowans were flourishing along the banks of the stream. The strawberry flower (Geum) hanging over the brook—all things soft and green.—In the afternoon William sat in the orchard. I went there, was tired and fell asleep. Mr Simpson drank tea, Mrs Smith called with her daughter. We walked late in the evening upon our path. We began the letter to John Wilson.

Sunday 6 June

A showery morning. We were writing the letter to John Wilson when Ellen came. Molly at Goan's child's funeral. After dinner I walked into John Fisher's intake with Ellen. She brought us letters from Coleridge, Mrs Clarkson and Sara Hutchinson. William went out in the evening and sat in the orchard. It was a showery day. In the evening there was one of the heaviest showers I ever remember.

Monday 7 June

I wrote to Mary H. this morning, sent the C. Indolence poem. Copied the letter to John Wilson, and wrote to my brother Richard and Mrs Coleridge. In the evening I walked with Ellen to Butterlip How and to George Mackareth's for the horse. It was a very sweet evening. There was the cuckoo and the little birds—the copses still injured but the trees in general looked most soft and beautiful in tufts. William was walking when we came in—he had slept miserably for two nights past so we all went to bed soon. I went with Ellen in the morning to Rydale Falls. Letters from Annette, Mary H. and Cook.

Tuesday 8 June

Ellen and I rode to Windermere. We had a fine sunny day, neither hot nor cold. I

Windermere, by Edward Dayes

mounted the horse at the quarry. We had no difficulties or delays but at the gates. I was enchanted with some of the views. From the High Ray the view is very delightful, rich and festive, water and wood houses groves hedgerows green fields and mountains, white houses large and small.—We passed two or three nice looking statesmen's houses. Mr Curwen's shrubberies looked pitiful enough under the native trees. We put up our horses, ate our dinner by the waterside and walked up to the station. Then we went to the island, walked round it, and crossed the lake with our horse in the ferry. The shrubs have been cut away in some parts of the island. I observed to the boatman that I did not think it improved. He replied: 'We think it is for one could hardly see the house before.' It seems to me to be, however, no better than it was. They have made no natural glades, it is merely a lawn with a few miserable young trees standing as if they were half-starved. There are no sheep no cattle upon these lawns. It is neither one thing or another— neither *natural* nor wholly cultivated and artificial which it was before. And that great house! Mercy upon us! If it *could* be concealed it *would* be well for all who are not pained to see the pleasantest of earthly spots deformed by man. But it *cannot* be covered. Even the tallest of our old oak trees would not reach to the top of it. When we went into the boat there were two men standing at the landing place. One seemed to be about sixty, a man with a jolly red face—he looked as if he might have lived many years in Mr Curwen's house. He wore a blue jacket and trousers, as the people who live close by Windermere, particularly at the places of chief resort, in affectation, I suppose. He looked significantly at our boatman just as we were rowing off and said, 'Thomas mind you take off the directions off that cask. You know what I mean. It will serve as a blind for them, *you* know. It was a blind business both for you and the coachman and me and all of us. Mind you take off the directions. A wink's as good as a nod with some folks'—and then he turned round looking at his companion with such an air of self-satisfaction and deep insight into unknown things!—I could hardly help laughing outright at him. The laburnums blossom freely at the island and in the shrubberies on the shore—they are blighted everywhere else. Roses of various sorts were out. The brooms were in full glory everywhere 'veins of gold' among the copses. The hawthorns in the valley fading away—

beautiful upon the hills. We reached home at three o'clock. After tea William went out and walked and wrote that poem,

'The sun has long been set' etc.

He first went up to G. Mackareth's with the horse, afterwards he walked on our own path and wrote the lines—he called me into the orchard and there repeated them to me—he then stayed there till eleven o'clock.

Wednesday 9 June

Wm slept ill. A soaking all-day rain. We should have gone to Mr Simpson's to tea but we walked up after tea. Lloyds called. The hawthorns on the mountain sides like orchards in blossom. Brought rhubarb down. It rained hard. Ambleside Fair. I wrote to Christopher and M. H.

Thursday 10 June

I wrote to Mrs Clarkson and Luff—went with Ellen to Rydale. Coleridge came in with a sackful of books etc. and a branch of mountain ash. He had been attacked by a cow. He came over by Grisedale. A furious wind. Mr Simpson drank tea. William very poorly—we went to bed latish. I slept in sitting room.

Friday 11 June

A wet day. William had slept very ill. Wm and C. walked out. I went to bed after dinner not well. I was tired with making beds cooking etc., Molly being very ill.

Ambleside marketplace, by John Harden

Patterdale, going towards Ambleside, by Thomas Allom

Saturday 12 June

A rainy morning. C. set off before dinner. We went with him to the Rays but it rained so we went no further. Sheltered under a wall. He would be sadly wet for a furious shower came on just when we parted.—We got no dinner, but gooseberry pie to our tea. I baked both pies and bread, and walked with William first on our own path but it was too wet there, next over the rocks to the road, and backward and forward, and last of all up to Mr King's. Miss Simpson and Robert had called. Letters from Sara and Annette.

Sunday 13 June

A fine morning. Sunshiny and bright, but with rainy clouds. William had slept better but not well—he has been altering the poem to Mary this morning, he is now washing his feet. I wrote out poems for our journey and I wrote a letter to my uncle Cookson. Mr Simpson came when we were in the orchard in the morning and brought us a beautiful drawing which he had done. In the evening we walked first on our own path. There we walked a good while. It was a silent night. The stars were out by ones and twos but no cuckoo, no little birds, the air was not warm, and we have observed that since Tuesday 8th when William wrote, 'The sun has long been set', that we have had no birds singing after the evening is fairly set in. We walked to our new view of Rydale, but it put on a sullen face. There was an owl hooting in Bainriggs. Its first halloo was so like a human shout that I was surprised when it made its second call, tremulous and lengthened out, to find that the shout had come from an owl. The full moon (not quite full) was among a company of steady island clouds, and the sky bluer about it than the natural sky blue. William observed that the full moon above a dark fir grove is a fine image of the descent of a superior being. There was a shower which drove us into John's Grove before we had quitted our favourite path. We walked upon John's path before we went to view Rydale. We went to bed immediately on our return home.

Monday 14 June

I was very unwell—went to bed before I drank my tea—was sick and afterwards almost asleep when Wm brought me a letter from Mary which he read to me sitting by the bed-side. Wm wrote to Mary and Sara about 'The Leech Gatherer'. I wrote to both of them in one and to Annette, to Coleridge also. I was better after tea.—I walked with Wm when I had put up my parcel on our own path. We were driven away by the horses that go on the commons. Then we went to look at Rydale, walked a little in the fir grove, went again to the top of the hill and came home. A mild and sweet night. Wm stayed behind me. I threw him the cloak out of the window. The moon overcast. He sat a few minutes in the orchard, came in sleepy, and hurried to bed. I carried him his bread and butter.

Tuesday 15 June

A sweet grey mild morning. The birds sing soft and low. William has not slept all night. It wants only ten minutes of ten and he is in bed yet. After William rose we went and sat in the orchard till dinner time. We walked a long time in the evening upon our favourite path. The owls hooted, the night hawk sang to itself incessantly, but there were no little birds, no thrushes. I left William writing a few lines about the nighthawk and other images of the evening, and went to seek for letters. None were come.—We walked backwards and forwards a little, after I returned to William, and then up as far as Mr King's. Came in. There was a basket of lettuces, a letter from M. H. about the delay of mine and telling of one she had sent by the other post, one from Wade and one from Sara to C. William did not read them. M. H. growing fat.

Wednesday 16 June

We walked towards Rydale for letters—met Frank Baty with the expected one from Mary. We went up into Rydale woods and read it there. We sat near an old wall which fenced a hazel grove, which Wm said was exactly like the filbert grove at Middleham. It is a beautiful spot, a sloping or rather steep piece of ground, with hazels growing 'tall and erect' in clumps at distances almost seeming regular as if they had been planted. We returned to dinner. I wrote to Mary after dinner while Wm sat in the orchard. Old Mr

Simpson drank tea with us. When Mr S. was gone I read my letter to William, speaking to Mary about having a cat. I spoke of the little birds keeping us company—and William told me that that very morning a bird had perched upon his leg. He had been lying very still and had watched this little creature, it had come under the bench where he was sitting and then flew up to his leg; he thoughtlessly stirred himself to look further at it and it flew onto the apple tree above him. It was a little young creature, that had just left its nest, equally unacquainted with man and unaccustomed to struggle against storms and winds. While it was upon the apple tree the wind blew about the stiff boughs and the bird seemed bemazed and not strong enough to strive with it. The swallows come to the sitting room window as if wishing to build but I am afraid they will not have courage for it, but I believe they will build at my room window. They twitter and make a bustle and a little cheerful song hanging against the panes of glass, with their soft white bellies close to the glass, and their forked fish-like tails. They swim round and round and again they come.—It was a sweet evening. We first walked to the top of the hill to look at Rydale and then to Butterlip How. I do not now see the brownness that was in the coppices. The lower hawthorn blossoms passed away. Those on the hills are a faint white. The wild guelder rose is coming out, and the wild roses. I have seen no honeysuckles yet except our own one nestling and a tree of the yellow kind at Mrs Townley's the day I went with Ellen to Windermere. Foxgloves are now frequent, the first I saw was that day with Ellen, and the first ripe strawberries. A letter from Coleridge. I read the first canto of 'The Faerie Queene' to William. William went to bed immediately.

Thursday 17 June

William had slept well. I took castor oil and lay in bed till twelve o'clock. William injured himself with working a little.—When I got up we sat in the orchard, a sweet mild day. Miss Hudson called. I went with her to the top of the hill. When I came home I found William at work, attempting to alter a stanza in the poem on our going for Mary which I convinced him did not need altering. We sat in the house after dinner. In the evening walked on our favourite path. A short letter from Coleridge. William added a little to the ode he is writing.

Friday 18 June

When we were sitting after breakfast, William about to shave Luff came in. It was a sweet morning. He had rode over the fells. He brought news about Lord Lowther's intention to pay all debts etc. and a letter from Mr Clarkson. He saw our garden was astonished at the scarlet beans etc. etc. When he was gone we wrote to Coleridge, M. H., and my brother Richard about the affair. Wm determined to go to Eusemere on Monday. In the afternoon we walked to Rydale with our letters—found no letters there. A sweet evening. I had a woeful headache, and was ill in stomach from agitation of mind—went to bed at nine o'clock but did not sleep till late.

Saturday 19 June

The swallows were very busy under my window this morning. I slept pretty well, but William has got no sleep. It is after eleven and he is still in bed. A fine morning. Coleridge when he was last here, told us that for many years there being no Quaker meeting held at Keswick, a single old Quaker woman used to go regularly alone every Sunday, to attend the meeting-house and there used to sit and perform her worship, alone in that beautiful place among those fir trees, in that spacious vale, under the great mountain Skiddaw!!! Poor old Willy—we never pass by his grave close to the churchyard gate without thinking of him and having his figure brought back to our minds. He formerly was an ostler at Hawkshead having spent a little estate. In his old age he was boarded or as they say *let* by the parish. A boy of the house that hired him was riding one morning pretty briskly beside John Fisher's—'Hallo! has aught particular happened,' said John to the boy. 'Nay naught at aw nobbut auld Willy's dead.' He was going to order the passing bell to be tolled.—On Thursday morning Miss Hudson of Workington called. She said, 'O! I love flowers! I sow flowers in the parks several miles from home and my mother and I visit them and watch them how they grow.' This may show that botanists may be often deceived when they find rare flowers growing far from houses. This was a very ordinary young woman, such as in any town in the north of England one may find a score. I sat up a while after William—he then called me down to him. (I was writing to Mary H.) I read Churchill's *Rosciad*. Returned again to my

Cottages at Portinscale, near Keswick, by Rev. Joseph Wilkinson

Eagle Crag, Borrowdale, by Cornelius Pearson

writing and did not go to bed till he called to me. The shutters were closed, but I heard the birds singing. There was our own thrush shouting with an impatient shout—so it sounded to me. The morning was still, the twittering of the little birds was very gloomy. The owls had hooted a quarter of an hour before, now the cocks were crowing. It was near daylight, I put out my candle and went to bed. In a little time I thought I heard William snoring, so I composed myself to sleep—Charles Lloyd called—'smiling at my sweet brother'.

Sunday 20 June

He had slept better than I could have expected but he was far from well all day; we were in the orchard a great part of the morning. After tea we walked upon our own path for a long time. We talked sweetly together about the disposal of our riches. We lay upon the sloping turf. Earth and sky were so lovely that they melted our very hearts. The sky to the north was of a chastened yet rich yellow fading into pale blue and streaked and scattered over with steady islands of purple melting away into shades of pink. It made my heart almost feel like a vision to me. We afterwards took our cloaks and sat in the orchard. Mr and Miss Simpson called. We told them of our expected good fortune. We were astonished and somewhat hurt to see how coldly Mr Simpson received it—Miss S. seemed very glad. We went into the house when they left us, and Wm went to bed. I sat up about an hour. He then called me to talk to him—he could not fall asleep. I wrote to Montagu.

Monday 21 June

William was obliged to be in bed late, he had slept so miserably. It was a very fine morning, but as we did not leave home till twelve o'clock, it was very hot. I parted from my beloved in the green lane above the blacksmith's, then went to dinner at Mr Simpson's. We walked afterwards in the garden. Betty Towers and her son and daughter came to tea. The little lad is four years old almost as little a thing as Hartley and as sharp too, they say, but I saw nothing of this, being a stranger, except in his bonny eyes, which had such a sweet brightness in them when anything was said to him that made him ashamed and draw his chin into his neck, while he sent his eyes upwards to look at you. His mother is a delicate woman. She said she thought that both she and her husband were so tender in their health that they must be obliged to sell their land. Speaking of old Jim Jackson she said, 'They might have looked up with the best in Grasmere if they had but been careful.' They began with a clear estate and had never had but one child, he to be sure is a half-wit. 'How did they get through with their money?' 'Why in eating and drinking.' The wife would make tea four or five times in a day and 'sec folks for sugar!' Then she would have nea teapot but she would take the water out of a brass pan on the fire and pour it on to the tea in a quart pot. This all for herself, for she boiled the tea leaves always for her husband and their son. I brought plants home, sunflowers, and planted them.

Tuesday 22 June

I had my breakfast in bed, being not quite well—I then walked to Rydale, I waited long for the post lying in the field and looking at the distant mountains,—looking and listening to the river. I met the post. Letters from Montagu and Richard. I hurried back, forwarded these to William and wrote to Montagu. When I came home I wrote to my brother Christopher. I could settle to nothing. Molly washed and glazed the curtains. I read the *Midsummer Night's Dream* and began *As You Like It*. Miss Simpson called— Tamar brought me some berries. I resolved to go to William and for that purpose John Fisher promised to go over the fells with me. Miss Simpson ate pie, and then left me reading letters from Mary and Coleridge. The news came that a house was taken for Betsy.

Aggy Fisher was talking with me on Monday morning 21st June about her son. She went on. Old Mary Watson was at Goan's there when the child died. I had never seen her before since her son was drowned last summer, 'We were all in trouble, and trouble opens folks' hearts.' She began to tell about her daughter that's married to Leonard Holmes, how now that sickness is come upon him they are breaking down and failing in the world. Debts are coming in every day and he can do nothing, and they fret and jar together. One day he came riding over to Grasmere—I wondered what was the matter and I resolved to speak to him when he came back. He was as pale as a ghost and he did not suffer the horse to gang quicker than a snail could crawl. He had come over in a trick of passion to auld Mary to tell her she might take her own again, her daughter and the bairns. Mary replied 'nobly (said Aggy) that she would not part man and wife but that all should come together, and she would keep them while she had anything.' Old Mary went to see them at Ambleside afterwards and he begged her pardon. Aggy observed that they would never have known this sorrow if it had pleased God to take him off suddenly.

I wrote to Mary H. and put up a parcel for Coleridge. The *Lyrical Ballads* arrived. I went to bed at half past eleven.

Wednesday 23 June

I slept till half past three o'clock—called Molly before four and had got myself dressed and breakfasted before five, but it rained and I went to bed again. It is now twenty minutes past ten, a sunshiny morning. I walked to the top of the hill and sat under a wall near John's Grove facing the sun. I read a scene or two in *As You Like It*. I met Charles Lloyd and old Mr Lloyd was upstairs—Mrs Ll. had been to meet me. I wrote a line to Wm by the Lloyds. Coleridge and Leslie came just as I had lain down after dinner. C. brought me Wm's letter. He had got well to Eusemere. C. and I accompanied Leslie to the boat house. It was a sullen coldish evening, no sunshine, but after we had parted from Leslie a light came out suddenly that repaid us for all. It fell only upon one hill, and the island, but it arrayed the grass and trees in gem-like brightness. I cooked C. his supper. We sat up till one o'clock.

Thursday 24 June

I went with C. half way up the Rays. It was a cool morning. I dined at Mr Simpson's and helped Aggy Fleming to quilt a petticoat. Miss Simpson came with me after tea round by the White Bridge. I ground paint when I reached home, and was tired. Wm came in just when Molly had left me. It was a mild rainy evening—he was cool and fresh, and smelt sweetly—his clothes were wet. We sat together talking till the first dawning of day—a happy time. He was well and not much tired. He thought I looked well too.

By John Harden

Friday 25 June

Wm had not fallen asleep till after three o'clock but he slept tolerably. Miss Simpson came to colour the rooms. I began with white-washing the ceiling. I worked with them (William was very busy) till dinner time but after dinner I went to bed and fell asleep. When I rose I went just before tea into the garden. I looked up at my swallow's nest and it was gone. It had fallen down. Poor little creatures they could not themselves be more distressed than I was. I went upstairs to look at the ruins. They lay in a large heap upon the window ledge; these swallows had been ten days employed in building this nest, and it seemed to be almost finished. I had watched them early in the morning, in the day many and many a time and in the evenings when it was almost dark I had seen them sitting together side by side in their unfinished nest both morning and night. When they first came about the window they used to hang against the panes, with their white bellies and their forked tails looking like fish, but then they fluttered and sang their own little twittering song. As soon as the nest was broad enough, a sort of ledge for them they sat both mornings and evenings, but they did not pass the night there. I watched them one morning, when William was at Eusemere, for more than an hour. Every now and then there was a feeling motion in their wings, a sort of tremulousness and they sang a low song to one another.

Tuesday 29 June

It is an uncertain day, sunshine showers and wind. It is now eight o'clock I will go and see if my swallows are on their nest. Yes! there they are side by side both looking down into the garden. I have been out on purpose to see their faces. I knew by looking at the window that they were there. Young George Mackareth is come down from London. Molly says: 'I did not get him asked if he had got his laal green purse yet.' When he went away he went round to see aw't neighbours and some gave him sixpence, some a shilling, and I have heard his mother say 't laal green purse was never out of his hand. I wrote to M. H., my brother Chrisr and Miss Griffith then went to bed in the sitting room. C. and Wm came in at about half past eleven. They talked till after twelve.

Wednesday 30 June

William slept ill, his head terribly bad. We walked part of the way up the Rays with Coleridge, a threatening windy coldish day. We did not go with C. far up the Rays but sat down a few minutes together before we parted. I was not very well. I was inclined to go to bed when we reached home, but Wm persuaded me to have tea instead. We met an old man between the potter's shed and Lewthwaite's. He wore a rusty but untorn hat, an

excellent blue coat, waistcoat and breeches and good mottled worsted stockings. His beard was very thick and grey of a fortnight's growth, we guessed, it was a regular beard like grey *plush*. His bundle contained Sheffield ware. William said to him after he had asked him what his business was, 'You are a very old man?' 'Aye, I am eighty three.' I joined in, 'Have you any children'. Children yes plenty. I have children and grand-children and great grand-children. 'I have a great grand-daughter, a fine lass thirteen years old.' I then said What, they take care of you—he replied half offended Thank God I can take care of myself. He said he had been a servant of the Marquis of Granby—'O he was a good man he's in heaven—I hope he is.' He then told us how he shot himself at Bath, that he was with him in Germany and travelled with him everywhere. 'He was a famous boxer, sir.' And then he told us a story of his fighting with his farmer. He used always to call me hard and sharp. Then every now and then he broke out, 'He was a good man! When we were travelling he never asked at the public-houses as it might be there (pointing to The Swan) what we were to pay but he would put his hand into his pocket and give them what he liked and when he came out of the house he would say, "Now they would have charged me a shilling or tenpence God help them poor creatures!"' I asked him again about his children how many he had. Says he 'I cannot tell you' (I suppose he confounded children and grand-children together). 'I have one daughter that keeps a boarding school at Skipton in Craven. She teaches flowering and marking, and another that keeps a boarding school at Ingleton. I brought up my family under the Marquis.' He was familiar with all parts of Yorkshire. He asked us where we lived. 'At Grasmere.' 'The bonniest dale in all England!' says the old man. I bought a pair of scissors of him, and we sat together by the roadside. When we parted I tried to lift his bundle, and it was almost more than I could do. We got tea and I was somewhat better. After tea I wrote to Coleridge and closed up my letter to M. H. We went soon to bed. A weight of children a poor man's blessing.

Thursday 1 July

A very rainy day. We did not go out at all, till evening. I lay down after dinner, but first we sat quietly together by the fire. In the evening we took my cloak and walked first to the top of White Moss, then round by the White Bridge and up again beyond Mr Olliff's. We had a nice walk, and afterwards sat by a nice snug fire and William read Spenser and I read *As You Like It*. The saddle bags came from Keswick with a letter from M. H. and from C., and Wilkinson's drawings, but no letter from Richard.

Friday 2 July

A very rainy morning. There was a gleam of fair weather and we thought of walking into Easedale. Molly began to prepare the linen for putting out, but it rained worse than ever. In the evening we walked up to the view of Rydale, and afterwards towards Mr King's. I left William and wrote a short letter to M. H. and to Coleridge and transcribed the alterations in 'The Leech Gatherer'.

Saturday 3 July

I breakfasted in bed, being not very well. Aggy Ashburner helped Molly with the linen. I made veal and gooseberry pies. It was very cold. Thomas Ashburner went for coals for us. There was snow upon the mountain tops. Letters from M. H. and Annette—A.'s letter sent from Gallow Hill—written at Blois 23rd.

Sunday 4 July

Cold and rain and very dark. I was sick and ill had been made sleepless by letters. I lay in bed till four o'clock. When I rose I was very far from well but I grew better after tea. William walked out a little I did not. We sat at the window together. It came on a terribly wet night. Wm finished 'The Leech Gatherer' today.

Monday 5 July

A very sweet morning. William stayed some time in the orchard. I went to him there. It was a beautiful morning. I copied out 'The Leech Gatherer' for Coleridge and for us. Wrote to Annette, Mrs Clarkson, M. H., and Coleridge. It came on a heavy rain and we could not go to Dove Nest as we had intended though we had sent Molly for the horse and it was come. The roses in the garden are fretted and battered and quite spoiled the honeysuckle though in its glory is sadly teased. The peas are beaten down. The scarlet beans want sticking. The garden is overrun with weeds.

Tuesday 6 July

It was a very rainy day but in the afternoon it cleared up a little and we set off towards Rydale to go for letters. The rain met us at the top of the White Moss and it came on very heavily afterwards. It drove past Nab Scar in a substantial shape, as if going Grasmere-wards as fast as it could go. We stopped at Willy Park's and borrowed a plaid. I rested a

Laundry, by John Harden

little while till the rain seemed passing away and then I went to meet William. I met him near Rydale with a letter from Christopher. We had a pleasant but very rainy walk home. A letter came from Mary in the morning and in the evening one from Coleridge by Fletcher. The swallows have completed their beautiful nest. I baked bread and pies.

Wednesday 7 July

A very fine day. William had slept ill so he lay in bed till eleven o'clock. I wrote to John, ironed the linen, packed up. Lay in the orchard all the afternoon. In the morning Wm nailed up the trees while I was ironing. We lay sweetly in the orchard. The well is beautiful. The orchard full of foxgloves the honeysuckle beautiful—plenty of roses but they are battered. Wrote to Molly Ritson and Coleridge. Walked on the White Moss. Glowworms. Well for them children are in bed when they shine.

Thursday 8 July

A rainy morning. I paid Thomas Ashburner, and Frank Baty. When I was coming home, a post chaise passed with a little girl behind in a patched ragged red cloak. The child and cloak—Alice Fell's own self. We sat in tranquillity together by the fire in the morning. In the afternoon after we had talked a little, Wm fell asleep, I read *The Winter's Tale*. Then I went to bed but did not sleep. The swallows stole in and out of their nest, and sat there *whiles* quite still, *whiles* they sung low for two minutes or more at a time, just like a muffled robin. William was looking at 'The Pedlar' when I got up. He arranged it, and after tea I wrote it out—280 lines. In the meantime the evening being fine he carried his coat to the tailor's and went to George Mackareth's to engage the horse. He came in to me at about half past nine pressing me to go out; he had got letters which we were to read out of doors—I was rather unwilling, fearing I could not see to read the letters, but I saw well enough. One was from M. H., a very tender affecting letter, another from Sara to C., from C. to us, and from my brother Richard. The moon was behind. William hurried me out in hopes that I should see her. We walked first to the top of the hill to see Rydale. It was dark and dull but our own vale was very solemn. The shape of Helm Crag was quite distinct, though black. We walked backwards and forwards on the White Moss path there was a sky-like white brightness on the lake. The Wyke cottage light at the foot of Silver How. Glowworms out, but not so numerous as last night. O beautiful place! Dear Mary, William. The horse is come Friday morning, so I must give over. William is eating his broth. I must prepare to go. The swallows I must leave them the well the garden the roses, all. Dear creatures!! They sang last night after I was in bed—seemed to be singing to one another, just before they settled to rest for the night. Well, I must go. Farewell.

On Friday morning, July 9th William and I set forward to Keswick on our road to Gallow Hill. We had a pleasant ride though the day was showery. It rained heavily when Nelly Mackareth took the horse from us, at the blacksmith's. Coleridge met us at Sara's Rock. He had inquired about us before of Nelly Mackareth, and we had been told by a handsome man, an inhabitant of Wytheburn with whom he had been talking (and who seemed by the bye much pleased with his companion) that C. was waiting for us. We reached Keswick against tea time. We called at Calvert's on the Saturday evening. On Sunday I was poorly and the day was wet, so we could not move from Keswick, but on Monday 12th July 1802 we went to Eusemere. Coleridge walked with us six or seven miles. He was not well and we had a melancholy parting after having sat together in

Keswick Lake, by Francis Towne

silence by the roadside. We turned aside to explore the country near Hutton John, and had a new and delightful walk. The valley which is subject to the decaying mansion that stands at its head seems to join its testimony to that of the house to the falling away of the family greatness. The hedges are in bad condition, the land wants draining and is over-run with brackens, yet there is a something everywhere that tells of its former possessors. The trees are left scattered about as if intended to be like a park, and these are very interesting, standing as they do upon the sides of the steep hills, that slope down to the bed of the river, a little stony bedded stream that spreads out to a considerable breadth at the village of Dacre. A little above Dacre we came into the right road to Mr Clarkson's after having walked through woods and fields never exactly knowing whether we were right or wrong. We learnt, however, that we had saved half a mile. We sat down by the riverside to rest and saw some swallows flying about and about under the bridge, and two little schoolboys were loitering among the scars seeking after their nests. We reached Mr Clarkson's at about eight o'clock after a sauntering walk, having lingered and loitered and sat down together that we might be alone. Mr and Mrs C. were just come from Luff's.

We spent Tuesday the 13th of July at Eusemere, and on Wednesday morning, the 14th, we walked to Emont Bridge and mounted the coach between Bird's Nest and Hartshorn tree. Mr Clarkson's bitch followed us so far. A soldier and his young wife wanted to be taken up by the coachman but there was no room. We had a cheerful ride though cold, till we got on to Stanemoor, and then a heavy shower came on, but we buttoned ourselves up, both together in the guard's coat and we liked the hills and the

Coach at Lodore, Keswick, by John Harden

rain the better for bringing us so close to one another—I never rode more snugly. At last, however, it grew so very rainy that I was obliged to go into the coach at Bowes. Lough of Penrith was there, and very impertinent—I was right glad to get out again to my own dear brother at Greta Bridge, the sun shone cheerfully and a glorious ride we had over Gaterly Moor. Every building was bathed in golden light. The trees were more bright than earthly trees, and we saw round us miles beyond miles—Darlington spire, etc. etc. We reached Leeming Lane at about nine o'clock, supped comfortably and enjoyed our fire. On Thursday morning, at a little before seven, being the 15th July we got into a post chaise and went to Thirsk to breakfast. We were well treated but when the landlady understood that we were going to *walk* off and leave our luggage behind she threw out some saucy words in our hearing. The day was very hot and we rested often and long before we reached the foot of the Hambleton Hills, and while we were climbing them still oftener. We had a sandwich in our pockets which we finished when we had climbed part of the hill, and we were almost overpowered with thirst when I heard the trickling of a little stream of water. I was before William and I stopped till he came up to me. We sat a long time by this water, and climbed the hill slowly. I was footsore, the sun shone hot, the little Scotch cattle panted and tossed fretfully about. The view was hazy and we could see nothing from the top of the hill but an indistinct wide-spreading country, full of trees, but the buildings, towns and houses were lost. We stopped to examine that curious stone, then walked along the flat common. It was now cooler, but I was still footsore, and could not walk quick so I left Wm sitting two or three times, and when he followed me he took a sheep for me, and then me for a sheep. I rested opposite the sign of The Sportsman and was questioned by the landlady. Arrived very hungry at Rievaulx. Nothing to eat at the miller's, as we expected but, at an exquisitely neat farmhouse we got some boiled milk and bread. This strengthened us, and I went down to look at the ruins—thrushes were singing, cattle feeding among green grown hillocks about the ruins. These hillocks were scattered over with *grovelets* of wild roses and other shrubs, and covered with wild flowers. I could have stayed in this solemn quiet spot till evening without a thought of moving but William was waiting for me, so in a quarter of an hour I went away. We walked upon Mr Duncombe's terrace and looked down upon the abbey. It stands in a larger valley among a brotherhood of valleys of different lengths and breadths all woody, and running up into the hills in all directions. We reached Helmsley just at dusk. We had a beautiful view of the castle from the top of the hill. Slept at a very nice inn and were well treated—bright bellows and floors as smooth as ice. On Friday morning the 16th July we walked to Kirby. Met people coming to Helmsley Fair—were misdirected and walked a mile out of our way—met a double horse at Kirby. A beautiful view above Pickering—Sinnington village very beautiful. Met Mary and Sara seven miles from Gallow Hill. Sheltered from the rain, beautiful glen, spoiled by the large house—sweet church and churchyard. Arrived at Gallow Hill at seven o'clock.

Friday 16 July

The weather bad, almost all the time. Sara Tom and I rode up Bedale. Wm Mary Sara and I went to Scarborough, and we walked in the Abbey pasture, and to Wykeham and on Monday the 26th we went off with Mary in a post chaise. We had an interesting ride over the wolds, though it rained all the way. Single thorn bushes were scattered about on the turf, sheep sheds here and there, and now and then a little hut—swelling grounds, and sometimes a single tree or a clump of trees. Mary was very sick, and every time we stopped to open a gate, she felt the motion in her whole body, indeed I was sick too, and perhaps the smooth gliding of the chaise over the turf made us worse. We passed through one or two little villages, embosomed in tall trees. After we had parted from Mary there were gleams of sunshine, but with showers. We saw Beverly in a heavy rain and yet were much pleased with the beauty of the town. Saw the minster a pretty clean building but injured very much with Grecian architecture. The country between Beverly and Hull very rich but miserably flat—brick houses, windmills, houses again—dull and endless. Hull a frightful, dirty, *brick housey* tradesmanlike, rich, vulgar place—yet the river though the shores are so low that they can hardly be seen looked beautiful with the

The marketplace, Hull, by Nathaniel Whittock

evening lights upon it and boats moving about. We walked a long time and returned to our dull day room, but quiet evening one, quiet and our own, to supper.

Tuesday 27 July

Market day. Streets dirty, very rainy, did not leave Hull till four o'clock, and left Barton at about six—rained all the way almost. A beautiful village at the foot of a hill with trees—a gentleman's house converted into a ladies' boarding school. We had a woman in bad health in the coach, and took in a lady and her daughter—supped at Lincoln. Duck and peas, and cream cheese—paid two shillings. We left Lincoln on Wednesday morning 28th July at six o'clock it rained heavily and we could see nothing but the ancientry of some of the buildings as we passed along. The night before, however, we had seen enough to make us regret this. The minster stands at the edge of a hill, overlooking an immense plain. The country very flat as we went along—the day mended. We went to see the outside of the minster while the passengers were dining at Peterborough—the west end very grand. The little girl who was a great scholar, and plainly her mother's favourite though she had a large family at home had bought *The Farmer's Boy*. She said it was written by a man without education and was very wonderful.

On Thursday morning, 29th, we arrived in London. Wm left me at the inn—I went to bed. Etc. etc. After various troubles and disasters we left London on Saturday morning at half past five or six, the 31st of July (I have forgot which). We mounted the Dover coach at Charing Cross. It was a beautiful morning. The City, St Paul's, with the river and a multitude of little boats, made a most beautiful sight as we crossed Westminster Bridge. The houses were not overhung by their cloud of smoke and they were spread out

Moonlight, a study at Millbank, by J. M. W. Turner

Dover from the Ramsgate Road, by W. H. Bartlett

endlessly, yet the sun shone so brightly with such a pure light that there was even something like the purity of one of nature's own grand spectacles. We rode on cheerfully now with the Paris diligence before us, now behind. We walked up the steep hills, beautiful prospects everywhere, till we even reached Dover. At first the rich populous wide spreading woody country about London, then the River Thames, ships sailing, chalk cliffs, trees, little villages. Afterwards Canterbury, situated on a plain, rich and woody, but the city and cathedral disappointed me. Hop grounds on each side of the road some miles from Canterbury, then we came to a common, the race ground, an elevated plain, villages among trees in the bed of a valley at our right, and rising above this valley, green hills scattered over with wood—neat gentlemen's houses. One white house almost hid with green trees which we longed for and the parson's house as neat a place as could be which would just have suited Coleridge. No doubt we might have found one for Tom Hutchinson and Sara and a good farm too. We halted at a halfway house—fruit carts under the shade of trees, seats for guests, a tempting place to the weary traveller. Still as we went along the country was beautiful, hilly, with cottages lurking under the hills and their little plots of hop ground like vineyards. It was a bad hop-year. A woman on the top of the coach said to me, 'It is a sad thing for the poor people for the hop-gathering is the women's harvest, there is employment about the hops both for women and children.' We saw the castle of Dover and the sea beyond four or five miles before we reached D. We looked at it through a long vale, the castle being upon an eminence, as it seemed at the end of this vale which opened to the sea. The country now became less fertile but near Dover it seemed more rich again. Many buildings stand on the flat fields, sheltered with tall trees. There is one old chapel that might have been there just in the same state in which it now is, when this vale was as retired and as little known to travellers, as our own Cumberland mountain wilds thirty years ago. There was also a very old building on the other side of the road which had a strange effect among the many new ones that are

Calais Pier, An English Packet Arriving, by J. M. W. Turner

springing up everywhere. It seemed odd that it could have kept itself pure in its ancientry among so many upstarts. It was near dark when we reached Dover. We were told that the packet was about to sail, so we went down to the Custom-house in half an hour had our luggage examined etc. etc. and then we drank tea, with the Honourable Mr Knox and his tutor. We arrived at Calais at four o'clock on Sunday morning, the 1st of August. We stayed in the vessel till half past seven, then Wm went for letters, at about half past eight or nine we found out Annette and C. chez Madame Avril dans la Rue de la Tête d'Or. We lodged opposite two ladies in tolerably decent-sized rooms but badly furnished, and with large store of bad smells and dirt in the yard, and all about. The weather was very hot. We walked by the sea-shore almost every evening with Annette and Caroline or Wm and I alone. I had a bad cold and could not bathe at first but William did. It was a pretty sight to see as we walked upon the sands when the tide was low perhaps a hundred people bathing about quarter of a mile distant from us, and we had delightful walks after the heat of the day was passed away—seeing far off in the west the coast of England like a cloud crested with Dover Castle, which was but like the summit of the cloud. The evening star and the glory of the sky. The reflections in the water were more beautiful than the sky itself, purple waves brighter than precious stones for ever melting away upon the sands. The fort, a wooden building, at the entrance·of the harbour at Calais, when the evening twilight was coming on, and we could not see anything of the building but its shape which was far more distinct than in perfect daylight, seemed to be reared upon pillars of ebony, between which pillars the sea was seen in the most beautiful colours that can be conceived. Nothing in romance was ever half so beautiful. Now came in view as the evening star sank down and the colours of the west faded away the two lights of England, lighted up by the Englishmen in our country, to warn vessels of rocks or sands. These we used to see from the pier when we could see no other distant objects but the clouds the sky and the sea itself. All was dark behind. The town of Calais seemed deserted of the light of heaven, but there was always light, and life, and joy upon the sea.—One night, though, I shall never forget. The day had been very hot, and William and I walked alone together upon the pier. The sea was gloomy for there was a blackness over all the sky except when it was overspread with lightning which often revealed to us a distant vessel. Near us the waves roared and broke against the pier, and they were interfused with greenish fiery light. The more distant sea always black and gloomy. It was also beautiful on the calm hot night to see the little boats row out of harbour with wings of fire and the sail boats with the fiery track which they cut as they went along and which closed up after them with a hundred thousand sparkles balls shootings, and streams of glowworm light. Caroline was delighted.

Calais, by William Owen

On Sunday the 29th of August we left Calais at twelve o'clock in the morning, and landed at Dover at one on Monday the 30th. I was sick all the way. It was very pleasant to me when we were in harbour at Dover to breathe the fresh air, and to look up and see the stars among the ropes of the vessel. The next day was very hot. We both bathed and sat upon the Dover cliffs and looked upon France with many a melancholy and tender thought. We could see the shores almost as plain as if it were but an English lake.—We mounted the coach at half past four and arrived in London at six the 31st August. It was misty and we could see nothing.

*Journal entry recording the marriage of William Wordsworth
and Mary Hutchinson*

We stayed in London till Wednesday the 22nd of September, and arrived at Gallow Hill
on Friday 24th September. Mary first met us in the avenue. She looked so fat and well
that we were made very happy by the sight of her. Then came Sara, and last of all Joanna.
Tom was forking corn standing upon the corn cart. We dressed ourselves immediately
and got tea—the garden looked gay with asters and sweet peas. I looked at everything
with tranquillity and happiness but was ill both on Saturday and Sunday and continued
to be poorly most of the time of our stay. Jack and George came on Friday evening 1st
October. On Saturday 2nd we rode to Hackness, William Jack George and Sara single, I
behind Tom. On Sunday 3rd Mary and Sara were busy packing. On Monday 4th
October 1802, my brother William was married to Mary Hutchinson. I slept a good deal
of the night and rose fresh and well in the morning. At a little after eight o'clock I saw
them go down the avenue towards the church. William had parted from me upstairs. I
gave him the wedding ring—with how deep a blesing! I took it from my forefinger where
I had worn it the whole of the night before—he slipped it again onto my finger and
blessed me fervently. When they were absent my dear little Sara prepared the breakfast.
I kept myself as quiet as I could, but when I saw the two men running up the walk,
coming to tell us it was over, I could stand it no longer and threw myself on the bed where
I lay in stillness, neither hearing or seeing anything, till Sara came upstairs to me and
said, 'They are coming'. This forced me from the bed where I lay and I moved I knew not
how straight forward, faster than my strength could carry me till I met my beloved
William and fell upon his bosom. He and John Hutchinson led me to the house and there
I stayed to welcome my dear Mary. As soon as we had breakfasted we departed. It rained
when we set off. Poor Mary was much agitated when she parted from her brothers and
sisters and her home. Nothing particular occurred till we reached Kirby. We had
sunshine and showers, pleasant talk, love and cheerfulness. We were obliged to stay two

hours at K. while the horses were feeding. We wrote a few lines to Sara and then walked out, the sun shone and we went to the churchyard after we had put a letter into the post office for the *York Herald*. We sauntered about and read the gravestones. There was one to the memory of five children, who had all died within five years, and the longest lived had only lived four years. There was another stone erected to the memory of an unfortunate woman (as we supposed, by a stranger). The verses engraved upon it expressed that she had been neglected by her relations and counselled the readers of those words to look within and recollect their own frailties. We left Kirby at about half past two. There is not much variety of prospect from K. to Helmsley but the country is very pleasant, being rich and woody, and Helmsley itself stands very sweetly at the foot of the rising grounds of Duncombe Park which is scattered over with tall woods and, lifting itself above the common buildings of the town stands Helmsley Castle, now a ruin, formerly inhabited by the gay Duke of Buckingham. Every foot of the road was, of itself interesting to us, for we had travelled along it on foot Wm and I when we went to fetch our dear Mary, and had sat upon the turf by the roadside more than once. Before we reached Helmsley our driver told us that he could not take us any further, so we stopped at the same inn where we had slept before. My heart danced at the sight of its cleanly outside, bright yellow walls, casements overshadowed with jasmine and its low, double gavel-ended front. We were not shown into the same parlour where Wm and I were; it was a small room with a drawing over the chimney-piece which the woman told us had been bought at a sale. Mary and I warmed ourselves at the kitchen fire. We then walked into the garden, and looked over a gate up to the old ruin which stands at the top of a mount, and round about it the moats are grown up into soft green cradles, hollows surrounded with green grassy hillocks and these are overshadowed by old trees, chiefly ashes. I prevailed upon William to go up with me to the ruins. We left Mary sitting by the kitchen fire. The sun shone, it was warm and very pleasant. One part of the castle seems to be inhabited. There was a man mowing nettles in the open space which had most

Wheat sheaves, by John Constable

likely once been the castle court. There is one gateway exceedingly beautiful. Children were playing upon the sloping ground. We came home by the street. After about an hour's delay we set forward again, had an excellent driver who opened the gates so dexterously that the horses never stopped. Mary was very much delighted with the view of the castle from the point where we had seen it before. I was pleased to see again the little path which we had walked upon the gate I had climbed over, and the road down which we had seen the two little boys drag a log of wood, and a team of horses struggle under the weight of a great load of timber. We had felt compassion for the poor horses that were under the governance of oppressive and ill-judging drivers, and for the poor boys who seemed of an age to have been able to have dragged the log of wood merely out of the love of their own activity, but from poverty and bad food they panted for weakness and were obliged to fetch their father from the town to help them. Duncombe House looks well from the road—a large building, though I believe only two thirds of the original design are completed. We rode down a very steep hill to Rievaulx valley, with woods all round us. We stopped upon the bridge to look at the abbey and again when we had crossed it. Dear Mary had never seen a ruined abbey before except Whitby. We recognized the cottages, houses, and the little valleys as we went along. We walked up a long hill, the road carrying us up the cleft or valley with woody hills on each side of us. When we *went* to Gallow Hill I had walked down this valley alone. Wm followed me. It was not dark evening when we passed the little public house, but before we had crossed Hambleton hills and reached the point overlooking Yorkshire it was quite dark. We had not wanted, however, fair prospects before us, as we drove along the flat plain of the high hill, far far off us, in the western sky, we saw shapes of castles, ruins among groves, a great, spreading wood, rocks, and single trees, a minster with its tower unusually

A prospect of York Minster, by William Fleetwood Varley

distinct, minarets in another quarter, and a round Grecian temple also—the colours of the sky of a bright grey and the forms of a sober grey, with a dome. As we descended the hill there was no distinct view, but of a great space, only near us, we saw the wild and (as the people say) bottomless tarn in the hollow at the side of the hill. It seemed to be made visible to us only by its own light, for all the hill about us was dark. Before we reached Thirsk we saw a light before us which we at first thought was the moon, then lime kilns, but when we drove into the market place it proved a large bonfire with lads dancing round it, which is a sight I dearly love. The inn was like an illuminated house—every room full. We asked the cause, and were told by the girl that it was 'Mr John Bell's birthday, that he had heired his estate!' The landlady was very civil. She did not recognise the despised foot-travellers. We rode nicely in the dark, and reached Leeming Lane at eleven o'clock. I am always sorry to get out of a chaise when it is night. The people of the house were going to bed and we were not very well treated though we got a hot supper. We breakfasted the next morning and set off at about half past eight o'clock. It was a cheerful sunny morning. We soon turned out of Leeming Lane and passed a nice village with a

A village green, by Thomas Rowlandson

beautiful church. We had a few showers, but when we came to the green fields of Wensley, the sun shone upon them all, and the Eure in its many windings glittered as it flowed along under the green slopes of Middleham and Middleham Castle. Mary looked about for her friend Mr Place, and thought she had him sure on the contrary side of the vale from that on which we afterwards found that he lived. We went to a new-built house at Leyburn, the same village where Wm and I had dined with George Hutchinson on our road to Grasmere two years and three quarters ago, but not the same house. The landlady was very civil, giving us cake and wine but the horses being out we were detained at least two hours and did not set off till two o'clock. We paid for thirty five miles, i.e. to Sedbergh, but the landlady did not encourage us to hope to get beyond Hawes. A shower came on just after we left the inn while the rain beat against the windows we ate our dinners which M. and W. heartily enjoyed—I was not quite well. When we passed through the village of Wensley my heart was melted away with dear recollections, the bridge, the little water-spout the steep hill the church. They are among the most vivid of my own inner visions, for they were the first objects that I saw after we were left to ourselves, and had turned our whole hearts to Grasmere as a home in which we were to rest. The vale looked most beautiful each way. To the left the bright silver stream inlaid the flat and very green meadows, winding like a serpent. To the right we did not see it so far, it was lost among trees and little hills. I could not help observing as we went along how much more *varied* the prospects of Wensley Dale are in the summer time than I could have thought possible in the winter. This seemed to be in great measure owing to the trees being in leaf, and forming groves, and screens, and thence little openings upon recesses and concealed retreats which in winter only made a part of the one great vale. The *beauty* of the summer time here as much excels that of the winter as the variety, owing to the excessive greenness of the fields, and the trees in leaf half concealing, and where they do not conceal, softening the hard bareness of the limey white roofs. One of our horses seemed to grow a little restive as we went through the first village, a long

Between Hawkshead and Coniston, by John Harden

village on the side of a hill. It grew worse and worse, and at last we durst not go on any longer. We walked a while, and then the post-boy was obliged to take the horse out and go back for another. We seated ourselves again snugly in the post chaise. The wind struggled about us and rattled the window and gave a gentle motion to the chaise, but we were warm and at our ease within. Our station was at the top of a hill, opposite Bolton Castle, the Eure flowing beneath. William has since wrote a sonnet on this our imprisonment—'Hard was thy durance Queen compared with ours'. Poor Mary! Wm fell asleep, lying upon my breast and I upon Mary. I lay motionless for a long time, but I was at last obliged to move. I became very sick and continued so for some time after the boy brought the horse to us. Mary had been a little sick but it soon went off.—We had a sweet ride till we came to a public house on the side of a hill where we alighted and walked down to see the waterfalls. The sun was not set, and the woods and fields were spread over with the yellow light of evening, which made their greenness a thousand times more green. There was too much water in the river for the beauty of the falls, and even the banks were less interesting than in winter. Nature had entirely got the better in her struggles against the giants who first cast the mould of these works; for indeed it is a place that did not in winter remind one of God, but one could not help feeling as if there had been the agency of some 'Mortal Instruments' which Nature had been struggling against without making a perfect conquest. There was something so wild and new in this feeling, knowing as we did in the inner man that God alone had laid his hand upon it that I could not help regretting the want of it, besides it is a pleasure to a real lover of Nature to give winter all the glory he can, for summer *will* make its own way, and speak its own praises. We saw the pathway which Wm and I took at the close of evening, the path leading to the rabbit warren where we lost ourselves. The farm with its holly hedges was lost among the green hills and hedgerows in general, but we found it out and were glad to look at it again. When William had left us to seek the waterfalls Mary and I were frightened by a cow. At our return to the inn we found new horses and a new driver, and we went on nicely to Hawes where we arrived before it was quite dark. Mary and I got tea, and William had a partridge and mutton chops and tarts for his supper. Mary sat down with him. We had also a shilling's worth of negus and Mary made me some broth for all which supper we were only charged two shillings. I could not sit up long. I vomited, and took the broth and then slept sweetly. We rose at six o'clock—a rainy morning. We had a good breakfast and then departed. There was a very pretty view about a mile from Hawes, where we crossed a bridge, bare, and very green fields with cattle, a glittering stream cottages, a few ill-grown trees, and high hills. The sun shone now. Before we got upon the bare hills there was a hunting lodge on our right exactly like Greta Hall, with fir plantations about it. We were very fortunate in the day, gleams of sunshine passing clouds, that travelled with their shadows below them. Mary was much pleased with Garsdale. It was a dear place to William and me. We noted well the public house (Garsdale Hall) where we had baited and drunk our pint of ale, and afterwards the mountain which had been adorned by Jupiter in his glory when we were here before. It was mid-day when we reached Sedbergh, and *market* day. We were in the same room where we had spent the evening together in our road to Grasmere. We had a pleasant ride to Kendal, where we arrived at about two o'clock. The day favoured us. M. and I went to see the house where dear Sara had lived, then we went to seek Mr Bousfield's shop but we found him not—he had sold all his goods the day before. We then went to the pot woman's and bought two jugs and a dish, and some paper at Pennington's. When we came to the inn William was almost ready for us. The afternoon was not cheerful but it did not rain till we came near Windermere. I am always glad to see Staveley it is a place I dearly love to think of—the first mountain village that I came to with Wm when we first began our pilgrimage together. Here we drank a basin of milk at a public house, and here I washed my feet in the brook and put on a pair of silk stockings by Wm's advice.— Nothing particular occurred till we reached Ing's chapel. The door was open and we went in. It is a neat little place, with a marble floor and marble communion table with a painting over it of the last supper, and Moses and Aaron on each side. The woman told us that 'they had painted them as near as they could by the dresses as they are described in the Bible', and gay enough they are. The marble had been sent by Richard Bateman from Leghorn. The woman told us that a man had been at her house a few days before who told her he had helped to bring it down the Red Sea and she had believed him gladly. It rained very hard when we reached Windermere. We sat in the rain at Wilcock's to change horses, and arrived at Grasmere at about six o'clock on Wednesday evening, the 6th of October 1802. Molly was overjoyed to see us, for my part I cannot describe what I felt, and our dear Mary's feelings would I dare say not be easy to speak of. We went by candlelight into the garden and were astonished at the growth of the brooms, Portugal laurels, etc. etc. etc. The next day, Thursday, we unpacked the boxes. On Friday 8th we baked bread, and Mary and I walked, first upon the hill side, and then in John's Grove, then in view of Rydale, the first walk that I had taken with my sister.

negus: hot spiced port and lemon

Saturday 9 October

William and I walked to Mr Simpson's.

Sunday 10 October

Rain all day.

Monday 11 October

A beautiful day. We walked to the Easedale hills to hunt waterfalls. Wm and Mary left me sitting on a stone on the solitary mountains and went to Easedale Tarn. I grew chilly and followed them. This approach to the tarn is very beautiful. We expected to have found C. at home but he did not come till after dinner. He was well but did not look so.

Mountain tarn, by John Harden

Tuesday 12 October

We walked with C. to Rydale.

Wednesday 13 October

Set forwards with him towards Keswick and he prevailed us to go on. We consented, Mrs C. not being at home. The day was delightful. We drank tea at John Stanley's. Wrote to Annette.

Thursday 14 October

We went in the evening to Calvert's. Moonlight. Stayed supper.

Friday 15 October

Walked to Ld Wm Gordon's.

Saturday 16 October

Came home Mary and I, William returned to Coleridge before we reached Nadel Fell. Mary and I had a pleasant walk, the day was very bright, the people busy getting in their corn—reached home at about five o'clock. I was not quite well but better after tea. We made cakes etc.

Sunday 17 October

We had thirteen of our neighbours to tea. Wm came in just as we began tea.

Monday 18 October

I was not very well. I walked up in the morning to the Simpsons'.

Tuesday 19 October

The Simpsons drank tea and supped. William was much oppressed.

Wednesday 20 October

We all walked on Butterlip How—it rained.

Thursday 21 October

I walked with Wm to Rydale.

Saturday 23 October

Mary was baking. I walked with Wm to see Langdale Rydale and the foot of Grasmere. We had a heavenly walk, but I came home in the toothache and have since that day been confined upstairs, till now namely Saturday 30th of October 1802. William is gone to Keswick. Mary went with him to the top of the Rays. She is returned and is now sitting near me by the fire. It is a breathless grey day that leaves the golden woods of autumn quiet in their own tranquillity, stately and beautiful in their decaying, the lake is a perfect mirror.

Saturday 30 October

Wm met Stoddart at the bridge at the foot of Legberthwaite dale. He returned with him and they surprised us by their arrival at four o'clock in the afternoon. Stoddart and W. dined. I went to bed, and after tea S. read in Chaucer to us.

Sunday 31 October

John Monkhouse called. Wm and S. went to Keswick. Mary and I walked to the top of the hill and looked at Rydale. I was much affected when I stood upon the second bar of Sara's Gate. The lake was perfectly still, the sun shone on hill and vale, the distant birch trees looked like large golden flowers. Nothing else in colour was distinct and separate but all the beautiful colours seemed to be melted into one another, and joined together in one mass so that there were no differences though an endless variety when one tried to find it out. The fields were of one sober yellow brown. After dinner we both lay on the floor. Mary slept. I *could* not for I was thinking of so many things. We sat nicely together after tea looking over old letters. Molly was gone up to Mr Simpson's to see Mrs S. who was very ill.

Monday 1 November

I wrote to Miss Lamb. After dinner Mary walked to Mr Simpson's. Letters from Cook Wrangham Mrs C.

Tuesday 2 November

William returned from Keswick.—he was not well. Baking day. Mr B. S. came in at tea time. Molly sat up with Mrs S. William was not well this evening.

Wednesday 3 November

Mr Luff came in to tea.

Thursday 4 November

I scalded my foot with coffee after having been in bed in the afternoon—I was near fainting, and then bad in my bowels. Mary waited upon me till two o'clock, then we went to bed and with applications of vinegar I was lulled to sleep about four.

Friday 5 November

I was laid up all day. I wrote to Montagu and Cook and sent off letters to Miss Lamb and Coleridge.

Langdale Pikes from Low-wood, by John White Abbott

Sunday 7 November

Fine weather. Letters from Coleridge that he was gone to London. Sara at Penrith. I wrote to Mrs Clarkson. Wm began to translate Ariosto.

Monday 8 November

A beautiful day. William got to work again at Ariosto, and so continued all the morning, though the day was so delightful that it made my very heart linger to be out of doors, and see and feel the beauty of the autumn in freedom. The trees on the opposite side of the lake are of a yellow brown, but there are one or two trees opposite our windows (an ash tree for instance) quite green, as in spring. The fields are of their winter colour, but the island is as green as ever it was. Mary has been baking to-day, she is now sitting in the parlour. Wm is writing out his stanzas from Ariosto. We have a nice fire. The evening is quiet. Poor Coleridge! Sara is at Keswick I hope.—William has been ill in his stomach but he is better tonight. I have read one canto of Ariosto today.

The mill, Grasmere, by Sarah Hutchinson

Friday 24 December, Christmas Eve

William is now sitting by me at half past ten o'clock. I have been beside him ever since tea running the heel of a stocking, repeating some of his sonnets to him, listening to his own repeating, reading some of Milton's and the 'Allegro' and 'Penseroso'. It is a quiet keen frost. Mary is in the parlour below attending to the baking of cakes and Jenny Fletcher's pies. Sara is in bed in the toothache, and so we are—beloved William is turning over the leaves of Charlotte Smith's sonnets, but he keeps his hand to his poor chest pushing aside his breastplate. Mary is well and I am well, and Molly is as blithe as last year at this time.

Borrowdale, by John Constable

Coleridge came this morning with Wedgwood. We all turned out of Wm's bedroom one by one to meet him. He looked well. We had to tell him of the birth of his little girl, born yesterday morning at six o'clock. W. went with them to Wytheburn in the chaise, and M. and I met Wm on the Rays. It was not an unpleasant morning to the feelings—far from it. The sun shone now and then, and there was no wind, but all things looked cheerless and distinct, no meltings of sky into mountains—the mountains like stone-work wrought up with huge hammers.—Last Sunday was as mild a day as I ever remember. We all set off together to walk. I went to Rydale and Wm returned with me. M. and S. went round the lakes. There were flowers of various kinds the topmost bell of a foxglove, geraniums, daisies—a buttercup in the water (but this I saw two or three days before) small yellow flowers (I do not know their name) in the turf a large bunch of strawberry blossoms. Wm sat a while with me, then went to meet M. and S.—Last Saturday I dined at Mr Simpson's also a beautiful mild day. Monday was a frosty day, and it has been frost ever since. On Saturday I dined with Mrs Simpson. It is today Christmas Day Saturday 25th December 1802. I am 31 years of age.—It is a dull frosty day.

· 1803 ·

Greta Hall, Keswick, by William Westall

Again I have neglected to write my journal—New Year's Day is passed Old Christmas Day and I have recorded nothing.—It is today January 11th Tuesday.—On Christmas Day I dressed myself ready to go to Keswick in a returned chaise, but did not go. On Thursday 30th December I went to Keswick. Wm rode before me to the foot of the hill nearest Keswick. There we parted close to a little water course, which was then noisy with water, but on my return a dry channel. We ate some potted beef on horseback, and sweet cake. We stopped our horse close to the ledge opposite a tuft of primroses three flowers in full blossom and a bud, they reared themselves up among the green moss. We debated long whether we should pluck and at last left them to live out their day, which I was right glad of at my return the Sunday following for there they remained uninjured either by cold or wet. I stayed at Keswick over New Year's Day, and returned on Sunday the 2nd January. Wm Mackareth fetched me. (M. and S. walked as far as John Stanley's.) Wm was alarmed at my long delay and came to within three miles of Keswick. He mounted before me. It had been a sweet mild day and was a pleasant evening. C. stayed with us till Tuesday January 4th. W. and I walked up to George M.'s to endeavour to get the horse, then walked with him to Ambleside. We parted with him at the turning of the lane, he going on horseback to the top of Kirkstone. On Thursday 6th, C. returned, and on Friday the 7th he and Sara went to Keswick. W. accompanied them to the foot of Wytheburn—I to Mrs Simpson's and dined and called on Aggy Fleming sick in bed. It was a gentle day, and when Wm and I returned home just before sunset, it was a heavenly evening. A soft sky was among the hills, and summer sunshine above, and blending with this sky, for it was more like sky than clouds. The turf looked warm and soft.

Saturday 8 January

Wm and I walked to Rydale—no letters. Still as mild as spring, a beautiful moonlight evening and a quiet night but before morning the wind rose and it became dreadfully cold. We were not well on Sunday Mary and I.

Sunday 9 January

Mary lay long in bed, and did not walk. Wm and I walked in Brothers' wood. I was *astonished* with the beauty of the place, for I had never been there since my return home—never since before I went away in June!! Wrote to Miss Lamb.

Monday 10 January

I lay in bed to have a drench of sleep till one o'clock. Worked all day petticoats—Mrs C.'s wrists. Ran Wm's woollen stockings for he put them on today for the first time. We walked to Rydale, and brought letters from Sara, Annette and Maggy—furiously cold.

Ambleside, by Francis Towne

Tuesday 11 January

A very cold day. Wm promised me he would rise as soon as I had carried him his breakfast but he lay in bed till between twelve and one. We talked of walking, but the blackness of the cold made us slow to put forward and we did not walk at all. Mary read the Prologue to Chaucer's tales to me, in the morning William was working at his poem to C. Letter from Keswick and from Taylor on Wm's marriage. C. poorly, in bad spirits. Canaries. Before tea I sat two hours in the parlour. Read part of 'The Knight's Tale' with exquisite delight. Since tea Mary has been downstairs copying out Italian poems for Stuart. Wm has been working beside me, and here ends this imperfect summary. I will take a nice Calais book and *will* for the future write regularly and, if I can legibly so much for this my resolution on Tuesday night, January 11th 1803. Now I am going to take tapioca for my supper; and Mary an egg. William some cold mutton—his poor chest is tired.

Shap Fell, by Peter de Wint

Wednesday 12 January

Very cold, and cold all the week.

Sunday 16 January

Intensely cold. Wm had a fancy for some gingerbread I put on Molly's cloak and my spencer, and we walked towards Matthew Newton's. I went into the house. The blind man and his wife and sister were sitting by the fire, all dressed very clean in their Sunday's clothes, the sister reading. They took their little stock of gingerbread out of the cupboard and I bought six pennyworth. They were so grateful when I paid them for it that I could not find it in my heart to tell them we were going to make gingerbread ourselves. I had asked them if they had no thick, 'No' answered Matthew 'there was none on Friday but we'll *endeavour* to get some.' The next day the woman came just when we were baking and we bought two pennyworth.

Notes on the Characters

For these notes on the more important figures mentioned in *The Grasmere Journal*, the Albion Press wish to acknowledge the assistance they have received from the earlier editions of William Knight (1897), Ernest de Selincourt (1941), Helen Darbishire (1958) and Mary Moorman (1971), from the biography *Dorothy Wordsworth* by Robert Gittings and Jo Manton (1985) and from notes compiled by Gordon Graham Wordsworth, the poet's grandson. They are particularly grateful to Pamela Woof for putting the results of her recent research at their disposal.

Ashburner: Thomas Ashburner and his family lived opposite Dove Cottage in Town End, Grasmere; he fetched the Wordsworths' coal from Keswick. His second wife Margaret ('Peggy') and his daughters Aggy, Jane, Molly and Sally are frequently mentioned as the Wordsworths' closest neighbours.

Baty: The Bateman or Baty family also lived in Town End; their house and land was known as Crag Top. It was up the road from Dove Cottage towards Rydale, and just north of the duck pond and How Top.

Benson: John Benson lived at Tail End, now Dale End, on the other side of Grasmere Lake. He owned Dove Cottage which until the early 1790s had been The Dove and Olive Bough Inn. The Wordsworths paid him £8 a year in rent.

Borrick: George Borrick (or Borwick) was the first landlord of the new inn in the centre of Grasmere, The Red Lion.

Calvert: William Calvert had been a schoolfriend of William Wordsworth at Hawkshead Grammar School; his younger brother Raisley was also at the school. The Calverts owned a farmhouse, Windy Brow, at Keswick, where Dorothy first shared a home with William in the spring of 1794. In the winter of 1794–5 William helped look after Raisley, who was dying from consumption. His generous legacy of £900, left to Dorothy and William, gave them some measure of financial independence.

Clarkson: Thomas Clarkson, the anti-slavery campaigner, and his wife Catherine lived at this time at Eusemere, near Pooley Bridge. Catherine became a close friend of Dorothy.

Coleridge: The poet, philosopher and critic Samuel Taylor Coleridge lived with his wife Sara and son Hartley at Nether Stowey, Somerset, in 1797. Dorothy and William moved to Alfoxden to be near them, and it was here, in 1798, that Dorothy first began to keep a journal. During the Wordsworths' first year at Dove Cottage, in 1800, the Coleridges moved to Greta Hall, Keswick, where their children Derwent and Sara were born. In her journal, Dorothy records not only the visiting and talking, walking and the work on the second edition of *Lyrical Ballads*, but also the anxiety about Coleridge's increasing unhappiness in his marriage and his poor health. After a trip to Malta in 1804 for his health (the single word 'Canaries' in Dorothy's journal for 11 January 1803 is a reference to Coleridge's abortive plan to go to the islands), he returned to Allan Bank, Grasmere, and tried to recapture his old intimacy with the Wordsworths. But his increasing dependence on opium was a difficulty, and by this time there were real differences in ideas. Nevertheless, William's verdict in later life, 'Coleridge was the only wonderful man I ever knew,' was true for him, and for Dorothy, from the first.

Cookson: The Rev. William Cookson was Dorothy's maternal uncle. When he married in 1788 he and his wife gave Dorothy a home at Forncett Rectory, Norfolk, until 1795.

Dawson: The Dawsons were close neighbours at How Top, along the road from Dove Cottage to White Moss.

Dockeray: Janet or Jenny Dockeray lived south of Butterlip How, off the road to Easedale.

Fisher: The Fishers lived at Sykeside, across from Dove Cottage and slightly to the south. Mary Fisher, known as Molly, was the Wordsworths' devoted servant; Dorothy wrote that she was 'honest and good as ever was a human being'. She lived with her brother John and his wife Agnes. After Agnes' death in 1804, Molly kept house for her brother alone, and the Wordsworths got a new servant. She died in 1808.

Fleming: Thomas Fleming kept The Hare and Hounds Inn at Rydale.

Fletcher: Fletcher, the Keswick carrier, who often brought and collected the Wordsworths' letters, had the house next to the Ashburners.

Gell: The young William Gell, later Sir William the archaeologist, had built a cottage on the other side of Grasmere Lake. The Wordsworths had the use of his boat when he was not at Grasmere.

Harrison: Anthony Harrison was a schoolfellow of William at Hawkshead Grammar School; he was a lawyer in Penrith and a minor poet.

Hutchinson: The Hutchinsons, like the Wordsworths, were orphaned in childhood, and lived variously with relatives. Mary, the eldest daughter, who married Wordsworth in 1802, had lived in Penrith with her mother's sister Elizabeth Monkhouse from the age of fifteen to eighteen. She then moved with her sisters Sara, Joanna and Margaret ('Betsy', who was mentally handicapped) to keep house for their brothers George and Tom at various farms in County Durham and Yorkshire. Dorothy Wordsworth lived for a time at Penrith with her grandmother; it was there that she and Mary became lasting friends. William met Mary when he paid visits, but they had first met as children at the same dame school. Coleridge met the Hutchinsons at Sockburn on Tees in 1799. He fell in love with Sara (the 'Asra' of his poems); the love, on both sides, was enduring and hopeless, for Coleridge was already married. Sara never married; she became a welcome aunt in all her relatives' and friends' families, and made her home mainly with Dorothy, William and her sister Mary Wordsworth.

Jackson: William Jackson built and owned Greta Hall, Keswick; Dorothy arranged for him to let half of it to the Coleridges.

Jones: The Rev. Robert Jones, a friend of William from his Cambridge days, had gone abroad with him in 1790.

Lamb: Charles Lamb worked for the East India Company in London. A schoolfriend of Coleridge at Christ's Hospital, it was through him that Charles and his sister Mary met and became lasting friends of the Wordsworths. Lamb tried his hand at poetry and drama before becoming in middle life the famous 'Elia' of the essays.

Lewis: Matthew Gregory Lewis was called 'Monk' Lewis after his Gothic novel *The Monk* (1796).

Lloyd: Charles Lloyd and his family came in 1800 to live at Old Brathay, near Clappersgate. He had published verse at twenty; had admired and even been a disciple of Coleridge, and had shared a volume of verse with Coleridge and Lamb in 1797. His relationship with Coleridge cooled, but he remained close to the Wordsworths: his sister Priscilla married William's and Dorothy's younger brother Christopher.

Lowther: In 1802, William, Lord Lowther, succeeded to his father the Earl of Lonsdale, and agreed to repay a longstanding debt of more than £8,000, which had been owing to William's and Dorothy's father.

Luff: Captain and Mrs Luff, originally friends of the Clarksons, had a house in Patterdale, but often stayed in lodgings in Ambleside to enjoy the wider society.

Mackareth: Dorothy knew two brothers of this name, both living in Grasmere: Gawen ('Goan') and George, the parish clerk, whose children George, Nelly and William are also mentioned.

Montagu: Basil Montagu, natural son of the Earl of Sandwich, met William in 1795. He became an eminent barrister, and William helped him to succeed: he lent him money, and relieved him for a time of the care of his small motherless boy, also Basil, who lived with William and Dorothy from 1795 to 1798.

Newton: Robert Newton kept the old Red Lion at Church Stile, Grasmere.

Matthew Newton was a local man who had been blinded in an accident at White Moss Quarry.

Olliff: The Olliffs or Olives, relative newcomers to Grasmere, lived at The Hollins. It is John Olliff whose delivery of dung is recorded in the same breath as William's composition of the 'Ode: Intimations of Immortality' on 27 March 1802.

Simpson: Two families of this name are mentioned. John Simpson and his wife Mary lived with her parents, the Parks, at the Nab, Rydale; their three eldest children were Margaret ('Peggy'), John and William. Margaret married the writer Thomas de Quincey and lived at Dove Cottage with him after the Wordsworths left in 1808.

The Rev. Joseph Simpson (or Sympson) of High Broadrain, Grasmere, was Vicar of Wytheburn; his wife, daughters and sons are mentioned frequently. Mrs Jameson is one of his daughters, and little Tommy is his grandson.

Southey: Robert Southey, when at Oxford, met Coleridge who was visiting from Cambridge; they planned an ideal society in America. They married two sisters and Southey, for the sake of his wife and Sara Coleridge, came to live in the other half of Greta Hall in 1803. He stayed for the rest of his life, looking after both his own and Coleridge's family. He and Wordsworth came to know each other well, and on his death in 1843 Wordsworth succeeded him as Poet Laureate. Southey was a prolific writer; *Thalaba*, a narrative poem in twelve books, was published in 1801.

Stanley: John Stanley was landlord of The King's Head at Thirlspot on the road to Keswick.

Stoddart: John Stoddart, later Sir John, became a well-known journalist and editor. He favourably reviewed *Lyrical Ballads* (1800) in the *British Critic* of February 1801.

Stuart: Daniel Stuart was editor of the *Morning Post* and the *Courier*, for which Coleridge was a valued, though erratic, ongoing contributor and Wordsworth an occasional one.

Vallon: Annette Vallon of Blois and William Wordsworth fell in love in France in early 1792; their daughter Caroline was born in December, by which time Wordsworth was back in England hoping to make money from publishing. War between England and France separated the lovers for ten years, and their passion subsided into friendship; nevertheless, William's and Dorothy's visit to Annette and nine-year-old Caroline in August 1802 was a necessary preliminary to his marriage to Mary Hutchinson.

Wilkinson: Thomas Wilkinson, a Quaker with a small estate and farm at Yanwath, near Penrith, was a recent friend of William Wordsworth.

The Rev. Joseph Wilkinson of Ormathwaite near Keswick, first mentioned on 31 March 1802, was an amateur artist; he asked Wordsworth to write the text for his *Select Views in Cumberland, Westmoreland and Lancashire* (1810). Wordsworth's contribution was anonymous, but became the basis for his later, signed *Description of the Scenery of the Lakes* (1822) and his subsequent *Guides*.

Wilson: John Wilson wrote an admiring critical letter to Wordsworth at the age of seventeen – and received a reply. A lively and athletic young man, he bought a cottage and small estate on Windermere and was often a summer visitor to the Lakes. As a reviewer and critic, he called himself Christopher North and was one of the first writers for *Blackwood's Magazine*. He became Professor of Moral Philosophy at Edinburgh University.

Wordsworth: Dorothy Wordsworth (1771–1855) was the third in a family of five children. Her four brothers were: Richard (1768–1816, solicitor), William (1770–1850, poet), John (1772–1805, sailor and sea-captain by the age of thirty of a leading ship in the East India fleet) and Christopher (1774–1846, clergyman and scholar, later Master of Trinity College, Cambridge).

Index of artists

Picture Credits and Acknowledgements

The illustrations in this book are reproduced by courtesy of:

Abbot Hall Art Gallery, Kendal: 22, 23, 29, 32, 36, 42, 46, 50, 52, 54, 58, 61, 64, 68, 70, 71, 74, 75, 76, 78, 79, 86, 93, 95, 97, 100, 102, 103, 117, 118, 139, 147, 152, 154, 157, 160, 168, 170, 172; Albion Press Ltd: 7, 14, 19, 33, 38, 40, 47, 48, 49, 55, 56, 60, 77, 81, 92, 99, 114, 116, 120, 121, 126, 128, 144, 145, 148, 149, 150, 155, 158, 161, 163, 165, 173, 187; Chris Beetles Ltd: 123; Birmingham City Museum: 87; Christie's: 125, 134, 159, 169, 181; Laing Art Gallery: 142; Mansell Collection: 27; National Gallery: 164; Private Collections: 39, 130, 141; Tate Gallery: 34, 108, 122, 162; Victoria and Albert Museum: 16–17, 25, 37, 43, 49, 51, 53, 59, 62–3, 65, 66, 69, 72, 80, 85, 88–9, 90–1, 94, 96, 105, 107, 110, 113, 129, 137, 138, 146, 151, 167, 175, 177, 178–9, 182–3; Wordsworth Trust, Dove Cottage: 5, 20, 30–1, 44–5, 57, 67, 83, 111, 119, 133, 166, 176, 180.

The Albion Press would like to thank all the above organisations for their help and cooperation in the making of this book. For special help they would like to thank Paul Allonby, Mr & Mrs C. Dunnington, Rosemary Hoggarth, Victoria Slowe (Director, Abbot Hall), Pamela Woof, Robert Woof (Hon. Secretary & Treasurer, Wordsworth Trust) and Jonathan Wordsworth (Chairman, Wordsworth Trust).